THE GIFT OF THE CHURCH

THE GIFT OF THE CHURCH

Msgr. Bob Guste

Forword by Fr. Benedict Groeschel, C.F.R.

NIHIL OBSTAT
Rev. Terry Tekippe
Censor Librorum

IMPRIMATUR
Most Reverend Francis B. Schulte
Archbishop of New Orleans

March 15, 1993

Library of Congress Catalog Card No: 93-083227

Published by:
Queenship Publishing Co.
P. O. Box 42028
Santa Barbara, CA. 93140-2028

Printed in the United States of America

ISBN: 1-882972-01-5

To
Long-standing and faithful friends

Tony and Joyce

Sign and Sacrament
of
Christ and His Church

ACKNOWLEDGEMENTS

My gratitude goes to many persons who have helped me with this book. Pat Alexander and Aggie Borne graciously did the typing and particularly Jackie Sigur, who was amazingly generous and great-spirited. Ramona Ford helped to check Scripture texts and Aida Cemalovic, the references. Dr. Joe Crapanzano and his wife Kay, Deacon Chris Bertucci and his wife Liz, John Kippley of the Couple to Couple League and pharmacists Paul Weckenbrock and Lloyd Duplantis and several brother priests helped critique or supply information for ch. 13 and the appendix. Jim Miller, Jean Gilfoyle and Didi Lagarde, of Human Life International, supplied the data on the question of population. Tony Viviano afforded great insights and gave me a couple of kicks in the pants to keep me going! Sisters of the Immaculate Conception, Germaine Delaune and Barbara Amedee helped check the manuscript. Frs. George Kosicki C.S.B.; Bob Vincent; Frank Montalbano O.M.I.; Geoffrey Graystone S.M.; Stan Klores; David Rabe; and especially Terry Tekippe gave valuable scriptural and theological help—and more. Adeline Brown, Adele Hughs, Marie and Anthony Nicolich, Raymond Calvert, Pastor Edgar Homrighausen, Mida Tuohy and Jeannette Bourgeois of the Clarion Herald, Diana Madonna of Loyola University's library, the staff of the New Orleans Baptist Seminary's library and of Concordia Lutheran Seminary's library, and especially Fr. Robert Stahl of Notre Dame Seminary's library graciously and patiently assisted with research. Special thanks also to Helga Whittaker, of Whittaker's Interpreters' Service, for the translation of Luther's letter and certainly to Fr. Benedict Groeschel for the foreword. I am also grateful to Janet Schaefer for the artistic work on the original and to Robert Frey for the current cover; Bob Schaefer, publisher, for his personal interest in the book and to John DeMers for putting me in touch with him - and for valuable literary suggestions as well. Of course there were others - including those who encouraged me and above all those who prayed for me, particularly my mother who at the age of 96 went to the Lord while this writing was getting ready to go to the publisher. To all - heartfelt thanks!

All Vatican Council II statements are taken from <u>Documents of Vatican II</u>, 13th. edition (American Press/Association Press, 1966), Walter M. Abbott, S.J., general editor.

All quotations from the Fathers of the Church, unless otherwise noted, are taken from <u>The Faith of the Early Fathers,</u> Vol. 1, selected and translated by William H. Jurgens (Collegeville, MH: The Liturgical Press, 1970).

Almost all biblical passages are from the revised edition of the New American Bible, copyright 1985, by Confraternity of Christian Doctrine, Washington, D.C..

When either the unrevised edition (copyright 1970, CCD) or another version is used it will be indicated in the text. The only exceptions are the subtitles to chapters seven and ten where the unrevised and the Confraternity of Christain Doctrine (copyright 1941) versions are respectively employed, without indication.

Words bold-faced from Scripture and other quotations indicated emphasis added.

———————————

Publisher's note:

About the Author

Msgr. Bob Guste, a diocesan priest of the Archdiocese of New Orleans, is presently engaged in a full-time ministry of evangelization and spiritual renewal. He has had wide pastoral experience in city, rural, suburban and inner-city parishes. His last pastorate was in a predominately African-American inner-city area of New Orleans. He has been engaged in many endeavors in behalf of interracial and social justice, respect for life, ecumenism, priestly fraternity and spiritual renewal. He is author of For Men of Good Will (1957) on race relations and the Church in Louisiana, Mary at My Side (1986, with a revised edition just republished by Queenship) a personal testimony about Marian devotion, and Come Home to the Church an outreach booklet for non-practicing Catholics. Fr. Guste hosts a local, Mon.-Fri. radio broadcast, "Living Waters", on WVOG,60 on the AM dial, at 6:30A.M., alternating weeks with Frs. Cohen, S.J. and Lafranz. He is also on world-wide shortwave radio 15.685 Mhg., Mon.-Fri. at 10:15 A.M., central time.

About Father Benedict Groeschel, C.F.R.

Father Benedict Groeschel, C.F.R. is director of spiritual development for the Archdiocese of New York. He is a psychologist, spiritual writer, seminary and university professon, retreat master and a widely known TV and video personality. Along with seven other friars he has established a new religious community called the Franciscan Friars of the Renewal, who work among the poor in New York's South Bronx. He is author of <u>Listening Prayer</u> (1984), <u>The Courage to be Chaste</u> (1985), <u>Stumbling Blocks or Stepping Stones</u> (1987), <u>Spiritual Passages</u> (1988) and <u>The Reform of Renewal</u> (1990).

TABLE OF CONTENTS

Foreword

by Father Benedict Groeschel, C.F.R.

When Our Lord Jesus Christ was preparing to "leave this world" and "return to the Father," He chose to leave His presence and message behind Him by a single powerful means. Despite what so many think, this was not a book, not even the New Testament. He left no book. We do not even have a piece of writing done by His own hand. For twenty years no writing that lasts to this day was written about Him. The oldest inspired Christian document is St. Paul's first epistle to the Thessalonians, written about 51 AD. The other writings inspired by the Holy Spirit would be written in the coming decades, along with many other devout works, often most valuable and authentic but which lack the mark of inspired Scripture. It was centuries before there was a book called the New Testament. Where did it come from? Who determined what writings would be in it? Where did it get its approval since Christ never mentioned any commentaries on His work such as the Epistles of John, Paul, Peter and others? An even more basic question is what held Christians together for those first centuries? What guided them in their interpretation of the sacred writings? What indicated that a particular teaching was false or erroneous? Who told them that certain interpretations agreed with the teachings of Christ and the Epistles and Acts written later by apostolic writers? What did the risen Jesus use as a means to guide His followers during the long centuries of persecution? What means did He use to authorize the sacred writings of Christianity and to guide His followers as new problems and questions arose? Who was to pass on baptism, the Eucharist, the forgiveness of sins by His power and the teaching authority of the apostles whom He assigned to carry on that mission in His name?

There is one single unavoidable answer to these questions, to all of these questions. He left the Church — His Church. The New Testament receives its authentication from the Church. The Church existed in embryonic form before the death of Christ. "On this rock I will build my Church and the gates of hell shall not prevail against it" (Mt 16:19 Confraternity version). Before the New Testament was formally published each document had to be approved as an inspired apostolic writing - by whom? By the Pope and councils of bishops (a word that comes from the Greek word for overseer) of the Church.

Without the Church there is no New Testament, baptism, Eucharist, laying on of hands, apostolic forgiveness, pardoning of sins. There is no authoritative teaching on the Virgin birth of Jesus, the meaning of the mystery of the Trinity, no clarity on the divinity of Christ, His physical resurrection or the second coming. These authoritative interpretations are all teachings of the ancient Church in the face of heresies or false ideas. Because the Scripture depends on the Church, in no place in the Old or New Testament is there any expression indicating that Scripture is the sole source of belief or interpretation (Sola Scriptura). On the contary St. Paul speaks of tradition or what has been passed on (2 Thes 2:15 & 3:6).

Christ told the apostles that those who listened to them were listening to Him. He also prophesied that the assembled community (another word for Church) would be persecuted, attacked and essentially would be in conflict with the world as He was; that it would be abused and betrayed as He was. He told them to expect to follow Him to martyrdom. And so for two thousand years, this is what has happened.

This book by my friend, Msgr. Robert Guste, is a powerful and popular statement about the Church founded by Jesus Christ. He pulls no punches about the difficulties that the Church is having in the present world situation. He confronts directly the prejudice and false ideas about the Church, even the lies repeated about the Church by people of good will. He bravely takes up the hard sayings, the teachings of the Catholic Church that are most unpopular - those concerning sexual morality. He shares with us his own struggles with the teachings which totally contradict what is PC or politically correct right now.

If you are a Catholic having trouble with the Church or a Christian of another tradition puzzled by this huge ancient Church that is so constantly attacked in the media and subject to endless vilification in the press - this book is for you. But if you like to be comfortable with your own lukewarm ideas and compromises with the world don't read another word. Knowing something accurate about the Catholic Church, as Msgr. Guste clearly indicates, will make you very uncomfortable. For those of good heart, on the other hand, <u>The Gift of the Church</u> should be received with great rejoicing!

INTRODUCTION

Are you enthusiastic about being a member of the Church? Does that "turn you on"? If not — why not?

To many, the Church is a problem — an obstacle — a stumbling block. They think that Jesus is great — and that their relationship with Him is "tight", it's OK, but the Church, ugh! They could do without her. And many do. They read the Bible, pray (even with others), do good, commit their lives to Jesus — but for the most part — or at least in a lot of ways — just bypass the Church. "The Church is for hypocrites!" Have you ever heard that one? Have you ever said it or thought it yourself?

Mystically — symbolically — the Church was born from the open side of Christ on the cross. She was purchased by the Son of God "with His own blood" (Acts 20:28). She is a precious, magnificent gift of the Savior to us. When is the last time you thanked Him for her?

She is meant to be "the light of the world — the salt of the earth" (Mt 5:13-14). You don't light a lamp and put it under a bushel basket or take the flavor out of the salt, but, somehow, some of us have been doing that in the Church. Are you and I part of the problem?

This book is about loving the Church, embracing the Church, getting excited about the Church, committing yourself to the Church — just as you embrace, get excited about, and commit yourself to Jesus Christ. It is about enthusiasm for the Church, hope for the Church, thanking God for the Church, standing on a mountain and inviting the whole world to come into the Church.

And it is by one who has had his own struggles with the Church, who, with sixty-six years of living and forty-two years of ministry as a priest, has seen many of the ups and downs of the Church — scandals, failures, arguments, bickering, pettiness, short-sightedness, etc., etc. It is by one who has had his own questions, struggled with his beliefs, committed his own sins, often failed to represent the Church properly, received his own hurts and suffered his own frustrations and discouraging experiences. It's written out of all this — and out of faith and love.

Feast of our Lady of Lourdes
February 11, 1993

Chapter 1

SURE THE CHURCH IS HUMAN BUT SHE'S ALSO DIVINE

"I don't go along with the *institutional* Church!"

How human the Church is! It's as human as you and I! In fact, the Church *is* us! Have you ever seen the word written this way: Ch -- ch? What's missing? U (you) R (are)! The Church is not made up of angels. She's made up of us, poor mortal men and women. And sometimes what a sad-looking lot we are! But that's God's plan for the salvation of the world. He chose human beings to continue His mission and He promised to be with us human beings until the end of time (Mt 28:20).

What a sorry-looking bunch were the apostles at times, so slow to understand and act! "Do you still not understand?" Jesus groaned (Mk. 8:21). One of them betrayed Him. All of them ran away the night He was taken. Peter denied he ever knew Him. Even after His resurrection, Thomas didn't believe until he had seen with his own eyes and put his finger in the place of the nails and touched His side. They were still asking when He was to restore the kingdom of Israel during the forty days. And on and on.

Paul and Barnabas had trouble working together. Peter and Paul had it out.

So what's new when we see the humanness, the conflicts, the sins in the Church today? He never promised a perfect Church. But He did promise His guidance to the Church as she continues His mission.

I met a man on a flight years ago. He was from Latin America and he was a writer. He said an interesting and amusing thing: "You know, when I run into people who criticize the Catholic Church, I like to say, 'Hey, if you had a history of two thousand years, you'd have a few skeletons in your closet too.'!"

Yes, our history is a history of 2,000 years. And in those years there have been a lot of things that we Catholics are not proud of, and a lot of them still happen today. Take the Inquisition, for example, the misuse of indulgences, or Popes who did scandalous things or the conduct of some Crusaders when they went to the East, or scandals among clergy today. The ship of the Church has passed through many dark days and troubled waters, but it's a Church that has lasted 2,000 years.

It was striking and significant that when Pope John Paul II came to our country, the newspaper and TV reporters and commentators, many of whom seemed to be anti-Pope, would repeatedly talk about "this Church of 2,000 years." They took it for granted. It's just a fact of history. Pick up any secular encyclopedia that's worth its salt and see if it says anything different. There is no other beginning in history for the Church to which we Catholics belong than with Jesus and Peter and the apostles. The story of the beginnings of the Church is right in the Gospels and in the

Acts of the Apostles (the Epistles and Revelation also). That's our roots. That's our story.

Other Christian Churches and denominations might say the same. But in honesty they have to add that somewhere along the line there was a break from the unity of the Church. For Orthodox Christians that happened in the 11th century; for Protestants in the 16th. After the Protestant break, with many Christians losing a center of unity and authority in the Catholic Church, there was an ongoing break away from those who broke and a spliting up into a multiplicity of denominations. In the beginning of the 20th century the Pentecostals represent such a split, but it still continues today. In fact, in modern times, in the last twenty-five or fifty years, for example, it is amazing how many new denominations have been started in the United States alone! By what authority? As someone put it, "When I hear somebody say, 'I started my own church,' my reaction is, 'I thought Jesus did that 2,000 years ago!'"

What the world needs is not another Church but the constant renewal of the Church Jesus established. The trouble with the Protestant Reformation was not that the baby didn't need a bath but that the original baby was thrown out with the bath water. The fact is that the baby *regularly* needs a bath — constant conversion and renewal until the Lord comes again. "...Christ loved the church and handed himself over for her to santify her, cleansing her by the bath of water with the word, that he might present to himself the church in splendor, without spot or wrinkle or any such thing, that she might be holy and without blemish." (Eph 5:25-27) Valid baptism, which cannot be repeated, is itself renewal in Christ Jesus. But it also signals the beginning of a *process* of dying to the old self and being continually "Christened" or renewed in Christ.

The Church is a mystery just like other mysteries of our faith — the Trinity, the Incarnation, the Resurrection. It's the mystery of Christ at work in the world through the visible sign or institution of His Church. We see the sign and the institution, but it's only with the eyes of faith that we can see Him at work in it and through it.

Even the word *institution* is a bad word for many people today. "I don't go along with the *institutional* Church," they say. Well what's so bad about the Church being an institution? Marriage is an institution — the most fundamental of all; so are the family, the school, the government, and even any social club. As long as we live in this world we're constantly forming and dealing with institutions. Every structured grouping of human beings is an institution. If the Church of Our Lord, Jesus Christ is going to exist *in this world* and carry out a mission, *it has to be an institutional Church*!

And as an institution it's got the hang-ups and problems of other institutions, but through it all Jesus continues His work in the world. To see Jesus and His Spirit at work in the Church takes the same kind of faith that it took to see God at work in and through the human nature of Jesus. Many failed to grasp that just as they fail to grasp the mystery of Jesus in His Church.

Addressing young people in Einsiedeln, Switzerland in June of 1984, John Paul II said, "I should like to ask you, dear young people, for two favors. First, be patient with the Church. The Church is always a community of weak and imperfect individuals... God has placed His work of salvation, His plans and His desires in human hands. This is indeed a great risk but there is no other Church than the one founded by Christ. He wants us human beings to be His collaborators in the world and in the Church, with all our deficiencies and shortcomings....

"And so my second request: Put yourselves at the disposal of the Church and work together according to the call you have received from Jesus Christ. Follow Jesus Christ! Put your lives in His service.... The Church needs you in many places, above all in the priesthood and in religious orders. You are the future of the Church. You yourselves are responsible for making the Church and keeping her young."[1]

"The Church needs you in many places" can be addressed to all members of the Church, the body of Christ. In marriage and single life, in hospitals and prisons, in business and politics, in medicine and recreation — wherever God has placed us, with all of our human limitations, there we are meant to be the extension of Jesus Christ, signs of His presence and instruments of His continued mission among us.

Sacred Scripture employs a variety of images in order to capture the rich mystery of Christ and His Church: a Shepherd and His sheep (Jn 10:11-15), a Bridegroom and His bride (Eph 5:23-32), a Head and His body (1Cor 12:12-31). Based on the Gospel scene of Jesus teaching from Peter's boat (Lk 5:3), the Church has also been called "the bark of St. Peter."

In her 2,000 year history, with all the things you and I have reason to be ashamed of, in faith we can say Jesus has never abandoned His Church. The Captain of the bark of St. Peter has never jumped ship. The Bridegroom of His bride, the Church, has never been unfaithful to that bride. The great Shepherd of His sheep has never run away when the wolves have come. And Jesus, the Head of His body the Church, has never separated Himself from His body.

The Church is truly the body of Christ. He has never gone back on His promise: "I am with you always, until the end of the age" (Mt 28:20). In all those troubled times and dark days, whenever that Church in the assembly of the bishops with their leader, the Pope, or through their leader alone, has found it necessary to raise her head in the world and to speak a clear and authoritative and sure word about what it is that God wants us to believe or do on the way to ultimate salvation — Jesus backs up His Church, "Whoever listens to you listens to me" (Lk 10:16). And, whenever that Church offers the sacraments of salvation: e.g., the forgiveness of sins, the anointing of the sick, the feeding of the flock with His very Body and Blood (no matter who the priest is, so long as he wants to do what Jesus and His Church want) then Jesus unfailingly forgives, Jesus anoints, Jesus feeds the flock with His Body and Blood. Jesus did His work in the world through His human nature. He continues that work through His body the Church. With all her humanity, her sinfulness, her short-sightedness, her pettiness, *the Church remains the chosen instrument of Jesus Christ to perpetuate His own ministry: to teach and sanctify, to unite and serve the world.*

Chapter 2

PROUD TO BE CATHOLIC

*"I don't believe in **denominationalism!**"*

'I've often told the story. It was when I was pastor of St. Francis de Sales, a predominantly black inner-city parish in New Orleans. We had sponsored a parish renewal weekend similar to those held in many parts of our country. The aim of the weekend was to develop a sense of Catholic identity and pride and, in the process, to heal past hurts and wounds within the community of the Church.

On Friday evening, as the program began, the participants were invited to express feelings about their membership in the Church and to air any grievances or hurts they had experienced (hopefully without defaming anyone). I can still hear the man who got up and said, "I don't go along with all this business of Catholic identity. I don't believe in **denominationalism**: 'I'm Catholic' or 'I'm Baptist' or 'I'm Methodist'. And, besides, I have objections and questions about the Catholic Church that no priest would ever be able to answer!"

I didn't say anything; but when I hear that, I feel like saying, "Hey, who started all the different denominations anyway? We Catholics didn't. It was those who broke from the mother Church, and they're still coming up with new ones today!" But the rules of the game were to let people say what they wanted, accept them where they were, love them, and let them participate in the whole program.

On Sunday morning, the final day, I was standing at the coffee table when my friend came over to me, "Hey Father, you remember what I said Friday night?" "I sure do," I answered. "Well," he said, "last night in our small group sharing (part of the weekend's method), a woman in our group prayed for me, and when I went home the Holy Spirit worked on me all night long. As I come back today, I just want to say how proud I am to be a Catholic! In fact I'm so proud that I want to put a sticker on my car saying, 'I'm Catholic and proud of it!'" "You're not going to find any stickers like that," I said. "Well," he said, "I'll have some made!"

Not long after, I left the parish and went off on a sabbatical in preparation for the full time evangelization and spiritual renewal ministry that I'm in right now. One day when I got back to town, I noticed on the bumper of a car right in front of me a sticker that said: "I'm Catholic and proud of it." The name of my former parish was on it.

I recall a statement back in the 60s, by one of the well-known Protestant observers at the Second Vatican Council, reported on the front page of our local Catholic newspaper. He said something to this effect: the Catholic Church is respected among the Christian denominations because of her clear and authoritative teachings, her sacramental life in which the mystery of Christ is continually celebrated and communicated, and her world-wide organization with its center in Rome. These are gifts of the Catholic Church to which many other Christians look with reverence. If this great Church, he went on to say, with her wonderful structure, could one day let in more fully the wind of the Spirit, then she could truly be the leader among all the Christian Communions.

A current writer, the brilliant and respected Richard John Neuhaus, when still a Lutheran pastor and theologian, in his 1987 book, The Catholic Moment, [1] sees the Church and Pope as having a providential role in the world and particularly in the U.S. at this critical time of history. He writes with a great respect for the work of John Paul II and Cardinal Ratzinger. As one reviewer of his book, Catholic Bishop Michael Sheehan, puts it: "He (Neuhaus) says that because of its dependence on rationalism, liberal Protestantism now has neither Scripture or Tradition. As a result, according to him, *the privileged place that liberal Protestantism used to have in U.S. thought is now gone. There is a vacuum.* And he says that *the Catholic Church has the opportunity to fill it, to make a serious contribution to American society with an influence that it never had before.*

"Neuhaus states that *religion is the sum total of the most binding ideas that people embrace in order to find meaning in life.* He proposes the incredibly inspiring, but critically challenging notion that *the Catholic Church can give such meaning to people's lives today.* Now Neuhaus doesn't say that we will succeed in the Catholic moment, merely that we have a chance to succeed. I believe that we will succeed only if and when we take evangelization seriously." [2] (Since writing his book, Neuhaus, himself, has more recently fully embraced Catholicism and been ordained a Catholic priest.)

We have enough examples of Jewish pride and Irish pride and Afro-American pride. What about some Catholic pride? The kind of pride I'm talking about is not a "holier-than-thou" attitude. The fact that I'm Catholic doesn't make me any better than my Baptist or Pentecostal or whatever brothers and sisters. So many of them seem to be closer to the Lord than so many of us Catholics. But the fact that I was baptized into the Catholic Church means that I have been given a tremendous privilege and a tremendous responsibility. What I do with it is what counts. I'll have a lot to answer for before the judgment seat of God. "Much will be required of the person entrusted with much . . ." (Lk 12:48). How much have I done with what I was given? How much have I let Him, in His Church, transform my life? How much have I shared with others all He has given me? That's what matters!

What the Second Vatican Council says about the Catholic Church is that *the fullness of what God wants for His Church is contained or "subsists in" the Catholic Church: the fullness of sacraments, of doctrine, of government and discipline.* In different degrees other Churches and ecclesiastical communities have some of these elements, but not to the same extent as Catholics. For example, some do not accept the Eucharist as the actual Body and Blood of the Lord or do not have valid ordination of priests or recognize the Pope as the legitimate successor of Peter. *Only in the Catholic Church do we have these elements all together.*

Precisely what the Council said is the following: *"This is the unique Church of Christ which in the Creed we* *avow as one, holy, catholic, and apostolic. After His resurrection, our savior handed her over to Peter to be shepherded (Jn 21:17), commissioning him and the other apostles to propagate and govern her (Mt 28:18 ff). Her, He erected for all ages as 'the pillar and mainstay of the truth' (1 Tim 3:15). This Church constituted and organized in the world as a society, subsists in the Catholic Church, which is governed by the successor of Peter and by the bishops in union with that successor, although many elements of sanctification and of truth can be found outside of her visible structure. These elements, however, as gifts properly belonging to the Church of Christ, possess an inner dynamism towards Catholic unity."*3

It's high time for us Catholics to quit hanging our heads as if we're ashamed of our Church and what she stands for. In ecumenical dialogues, if we continually don't refer to the things that make us unique, then what do we have that will enrich the sharing? It's what they call "sloppy agape" when we act as if we're already one when, in fact, we're not. Let's share what we have in common as well as our differences openly and honestly and lovingly when the occasion warrants it. Most Protestants want us Catholics to be ourselves and to be true to ourselves. And they will respect us all the more for that. And then, let God do the rest.

There are a lot of sharing groups and fellowships around that propose to be non-denominational or inter-denominational. They meet regularly for prayer, Bible reading, witnessing and mutual encouragement. Their coming together could have great personal and ecumenical benefit. I am concerned, however, about the long-term effect such groups may have on many people, especially Catholics. Understandably, these associations usually make a decided effort to avoid the discussion of certain doctrines of faith (though inevitably you need to talk about doctrines if you're talking about Jesus Christ, the Bible and salvation). References to Catholic beliefs about the Eucharist, the Pope, or devotion to Mary and the saints would be considered out of place. Because of this regular omission, some members could begin to think after a while that all of that is really not important; it's just window dressing, and those who bring it up are "old fashioned" or "narrow."

As Catholics, we have a special treasure. It's Jesus with the richness of all He wants to share with us in His body the Church. He, with His Church, is the Light of the world. Let's not hide that light under a bushel basket but let it shine brightly for all to see. Let's share it with a world that still walks in so much darkness!

After a parish mission in which I stressed the gift of the Church and the need to share that gift with everyone, a man wrote me this simple story. He said that because of the mission he was inspired to go see a friend (we'll call him Joe) who was a veteran and an invalid. It was someone he had visited off and on in the past, but this time he had the courage to ask him if he was interested in receiving instructions in the Catholic faith. (He had never been baptized in any denomination even though his wife and family were Catholic.)

"No," Joe said, "I'm not interested." So he didn't push the issue. Before he left, however, he asked Joe if he were willing to pray with him. When Joe said okay, my friend told me: "I just prayed an Our Father with him. Right after the prayer I asked him once again and Joe said, 'Hey, you know I think I would be interested in receiving instructions.'" He arranged to have the parish priest come to see him. He was instructed, baptized, made his first Communion, was anointed, and not too long after that, the Lord took him home...

"As each one has received a gift, use it to serve one another as good stewards of God's varied grace" (1 Pt 4:10). *The greatest gift we have to share is our faith in Christ and His Church. To share our faith is to share the greatest treasure.* Let's do that first of all with those who have drifted from the Catholic Church, then with those who are unchurched — but also with all who are open to the truth.

GIFT OF THE CHURCH

Chapter 3

JESUS AND HIS CHURCH

"I found Jesus Christ and I left the Catholic Church!"

"I found Jesus Christ and I left the Catholic Church!" Have you ever heard that one? Surely, I have. What's it all about? Why does it happen?

Everything in the Catholic Church has a central focus. Do you know what that focus is? Do you know the center, the purpose of it all? *The center, the focus, the purpose of the Catholic Church is our Lord Jesus Christ*. That He might be "lifted up" (Jn 12:32) for all the nations to see, to know, to love, to accept and follow as true Lord of the world and of the lives of every one of us — everything we do in the Catholic Church is meant to be for that. The Church is all about Jesus and our ever-deepening relationship with Him, our openness to Him and His Spirit so that we can together continue His mission.

That's the way it's supposed to be — but do we Catholics always realize it or do we priests always emphasize it? Obviously not.

Let me just tell my own story. I grew up learning about Jesus — at home, in school, and in church. I knew that He was the most important person who ever lived and was meant to be the most important person in my life. But I didn't think that much about my own personal relationship with Him — even in the early years of my life as a priest.

As a young priest, I threw myself into the thick of parish ministry and became busy about many things. I was working with youth, meeting regularly with groups of married couples in the exciting new Christian Family Movement, and I was concerned and active with issues of social and interracial justice and peace, especially in the life of the Church.

But I noticed as the years went along that deep down in my own heart there was a restlessness, a hunger, a lack of peace. I went through a long time of spiritual direction, of searching, of counselling to try to find out what was wrong, what was missing. For a while I thought that maybe I shouldn't be a priest, that I had missed my vocation. This soul-searching however helped me get in touch with some of my own unrealistic expectations, fears and neurotic compulsions; but most of all I came to understand that the main thing that was missing was my personal relationship with Jesus. Every human being (knowingly or unknowingly) longs for personal relationships. We seek them in friendships and in marriage, but back of it all is the desire (known or unknown) for that ultimate relationship with God, with Jesus Christ.

I knew Jesus. I loved Him. I was trying to follow Him. I didn't know Him, however, in a deep, personal way. I didn't know Him the way a friend knows a friend, the way that a good husband and wife are meant to know one another. I didn't know Jesus in that way. I didn't love Him in that way. But I realized then, about ten years after ordination, that if I were to go on ministering as a priest, that that had to change. That hunger in my heart had to be filled by Him who called Himself "the bread of life," and who said, "whoever comes to me will never hunger, and whoever believes in me will never thirst" (Jn 6:35). I knew then that there were hungers in my heart that He alone could fill — that there was a thirst inside me that He alone, the source of "living water" (Jn 4:10), could quench.

I was an assistant in a downtown parish. I had my duties. But in the midst of them, I made a commitment to stop being "too busy," cut out some unnecessary things and, for a year, to seek one thing above all — to deepen my relationship with Him.

The first thing I knew I had to do to make that possible was to *take more time each day to pray*. What's missing in so many relationships and so many marriages is communication, taking time for it and being honest in it. I realized then that I needed more honest communication with the Lord. I needed to open up, lay out my whole life before Him and allow Him to do in me or say to me all that He wanted. As I began to do that, to take a good chunk of time each day (at least an hour) especially in the presence of our Lord in the Blessed Sacrament, I found it tough! Time and time again I didn't want to be there. I wanted to run. I could think of all the other things that I thought I had to do or wanted to do. But, as I went back day after day, He convinced me that the main thing that I had to do, that I needed to do, was pray. (I was learning that when you're too busy to pray, you're *too busy*!) What I experienced as I "sweated it out" in His presence was that I was sweating out the things that were barriers between me and Him.

I think about something that I read years ago in an introduction to a book on prayer by Thomas Merton. The introduction says that prayer is something like the old theater houses where there used to be three curtains. One curtain would go up and then the second and finally the third, and you were face to face with the players. Prayer is something like that. As we go back to pray day after day in the course of our lives, little by little, almost imperceptibly, the barriers, the defenses between ourselves and the Lord come down, and we're more and more face to face with Him.

I experienced something like that as I went back to prayer again and again. I realized that what I was sweating out were a lot of things that I had not faced before, that I didn't even know about: my pride, self-centeredness, laziness, self-indulgence and so on down the line. He was breaking through; walls were coming down.

Secondly, the thing I did that year was to **read the Bible** in a new way. Everybody who prepares for the priesthood studies the Scriptures deeply, and I had studied them. It was also a required part of our seminary rule that every day we would take at least fifteen minutes to read the Bible. I did that, but I did it mechanically. I did it because I had to do it. But that year of my life, ten years after ordination, I did it because I wanted to do it — because I was hungry for God. Jerome a saint of the Catholic Church, lived three hundred years after Christ and spent much of his life poring over the Scriptures and translating them to make them available to the people of his day. Jerome said, "Ignorance of the

Scriptures is ignorance of Jesus." I didn't want to be igno-
rant of Him.

As I read the Scriptures day after day, as I took more
time for that, there were days when it was uninteresting,
when I read passages that had little meaning for my life. But
as I continued to read, like lights on a dark street, the words
took on new meaning, and I realized that what I was reading
was not just the story of something that had happened a
long time ago. Through the words and the events of Scripture, God was speaking to me right now; God was touching
my life! I began to see the relationship between what I was
reading and what was happening around me and within me,
and I started to write down these thoughts.

Thirdly, what I did (at least for that year) was to *practice
a little more self-discipline*, especially in the way of eating.
I come from an "eating" family, a restaurant family. Even to
make some small sacrifices in that regard was a big thing
for me! What I experienced, however, was what the Scriptures and the tradition and history of the Church tell us.
There is an intimate connection between fasting, or whatever type of self-denial or self-discipline we choose, and
opening our hearts to God.

When that year was over, I experienced a new peace in
my life. When I lose it now, I know where to find it. I find
it in Him who is the Prince of Peace (Is 9:5), the source of
our peace.

There was a new relationship with Him — **as *my
brother and friend, my Savior and the Lord of my life*.** I
realized also that what I had begun was a journey, not for a
day, not for a month, not for a year, but for a lifetime. As the
old song from the musical "Godspell" puts it: "to see thee
more clearly, love thee more dearly, and follow thee more

nearly day by day." And I realized better than I had ever realized before the simple truth that the center of everything that I was doing as a priest and everything we do as Catholic Christians is — Our Lord Jesus Christ. Everything in the Church revolves around Him. *Every sacrament of the Church is a meeting with Jesus under a sacred sign.*

Jesus isn't walking among us the same way He walked among the people of Galilee or Palestine, but because we're human beings, we want to be able to see and touch and hear something; we want to contact God in a down-to-earth concrete way. God knows that we want this, that in a certain sense we even need it. And that's the reason (or at least one of the reasons) for the Incarnation — Jesus Christ, God in the flesh. And that's the reason for the Church and the sacraments — those sacred signs of His presence, His working among us.

Every one of those seven sacraments is a meeting with Jesus Christ. He's what they're all about. In baptism, He's the one who immerses us in His death and resurrection and joins us to His body the Church. In reconciliation, He's the one who again reconciles us to the Father and to one another through His Church. In the anointing of the sick, He's the one whose healing power is going out. He's the one imparting the gift of the Holy Spirit to those confirmed, ordained to the ministry, or joined together in marriage. Especially, in the sacrament of sacraments, the Holy Eucharist, He's the one calling us over and over again to unite ourselves to His eternal surrender to the Father and feeding us with His own Body and Blood. Every sacrament is a meeting with Him and a celebration in the community of the Church of the dying and rising of the Lord. It is a celebration of the entire work and mystery of Jesus Christ.

Every teaching of the Church is connected with Our Blessed Lord. Whether it's about eternal life, grace, salvation, about the Church herself, the sacraments, or how to live in this world, all of it is connected with Our Lord at the center. *Every law of the Church is also centered in Him.*

Why do we have laws in the Church anyway? Every family, every organization, every group of people that wants to stay together and be committed to some work needs leadership, needs legitimate authority and some rules or regulations to hold them together. Our Catholic family spread out around the earth is no exception. But this leadership, this authority, these rules are there for a purpose. They're there to hold us together with one another around Our Lord, Jesus Christ, our Head — that together we might continue His mission.

Every devotion in the Church, no matter what, *is related to Jesus.* Take for example the devotion to the saints. Why do we honor the saints? We honor them for a simple reason. They were men, women, and young people like ourselves. They were black and white, yellow and red. They lived in all different circumstances, in all different parts of the world, in all different cultures. They put up with all the troubles and difficulties that you and I put up with, with all the ups and downs. They had the temptations that you and I have, and sometimes they fell along the way. But through it all they tried to follow Jesus. They tried to make Him the Lord and center of their lives and proclaim Him to others. And the Church honors them in order to say to us, "Hey! Following Jesus is for us real live human beings of today. They did it and you can do it. And, they're that mighty company of witnesses pulling for you, praying for you and saying 'hang in there, baby, we made it and you can make it too'!"

What I'm saying is this. Sometimes we're like people who miss the forest for the trees. The trees are the sacraments, the teachings, the laws, the devotions. They're beautiful; they're important; they're needed. Appreciate them. Don't neglect them. They're there for a purpose. They are there to lead us to an ever deepening relationship with Our Lord Jesus Christ at the center. They're there that we might grow in knowing Him, loving Him, and surrendering ourselves to Him so that He might become more and more the Lord of our lives and use us to continue His mission. He's the forest. They're the trees. Don't miss Him through it all.

Ideal Catholics held up to us by the Church are the *saints*. As you read their lives, what do you notice? One after the other, ***they were men and women who had a deep, personal relationship with Our Lord Jesus Christ***. Their hearts were on fire with love for Him. Take a man like Ignatius of Loyola. The religious community he founded was originally called the Company of Jesus (in line with his military background). Alphonsus Ligouri, with his brilliant mind, composed that prayer I learned as a child in Catholic school: "I love You Jesus, my love. I love You more than myself. I repent with my whole heart for ever having offended you. Grant that I may love You always and then do with me what is Your will." A woman like Margaret Mary, to whom Our Lord appeared with His heart ablaze with love, spent her life proclaiming the mystery of Jesus' personal love for each of us. Therese, called "the little flower of Jesus," died at the young age of 24. Under obedience, she wrote her autobiography, The Story of a

Soul. Every page burns with love for Our Lord. One after the other, these men and women had a deep personal love for Jesus — and as a result, an ever growing love for all their sisters and brothers.

Sometimes for us Catholics, when we read these lives or hear them we think, "Well, that was okay for them but it's not for me." The Church honors them in order to say, "Hey! It is for *you!*" We're all called to genuine holiness, as the Second Vatican Council reminds us. We're all called to grow every day in knowing, loving and serving Our Lord, Jesus Christ. That's our goal, and everything we do in the Church is meant to foster that goal.

Today, unfortunately, we find the phenomenon of those who say, "Well, I left the Catholic Church. I went to some other church. I heard this program on the radio. I talked to this man or woman at work — and I found Jesus Christ." There's no doubt about it some people do find a break-through in their relationship or their lack of relationship with the Lord in ways like this. Thank God for what they find. But that's no reason to leave the Catholic Church. The Catholic Church is all about Jesus and *if you've found a new relationship with Him, now foster it within that Mother Church to which God wants you to belong.*

That breakthrough in the relationship with Him could happen in a thousand different ways. For many people it happens at the time of Holy Communion or during confession or when hearing a sermon or while participating in a prayer meeting, a retreat or "Life in the Spirit Seminar", a weekend Cursillo or Marriage Encounter. For many others it has happened on a hospital bed or in the midst of a tragedy or at the time of a separation or breakup of a marriage or while looking at a beautiful sunset or on a battlefield or on a vacation. The moment of grace can come at any time, but because it might happen on the occasion when a Catholic is talking to or meeting with persons who are not Catholic does not mean that God is calling that person out of the Church. God is everywhere. He can use a thousand different ways and people to touch our lives; but that's not the final determinant of where He wants us to put our allegiance as members of His Church.

When I rediscovered Jesus in His Church and realized more clearly how He is the one who stands behind everything we do, I began to meet Him over and over again in the midst of the activities of the Church. I meet Him especially in the activity that I try to participate in every day: the Holy Eucharist. *In this world there is absolutely no greater sign and instrument of His intimacy with us than the Holy Eucharist.* I believe that when I participate in the Eucharistic sacrifice, I am intimately joining myself with Him in His surrender to the Father and that when I go to Holy Communion, He is coming to me not just spiritually but with His very Body and Blood. Jesus, the risen Lord, is meeting me in His fullness in this wonderful sacrament. He's inviting me to open my whole life to Him, to let Him be the center of my life, to warm my heart with His love and to fill me with His Spirit and the power of His Resurrection. And He sends me out to the world day after day to bring that love, that healing, that power of His Resurrection to every person and every aspect of life.

Sure, I've gone to Mass at times with negative thoughts and feelings, distracted and saddened about things that were happening in the world, the Church, or in myself, critical maybe of the homily (sometimes my own!) or the liturgy of the very Mass I was concelebrating with brother priests. I was having trouble seeing the face of Jesus in His Church. Then it happened. Communion time came and my heart melted and all the rest seemed to fade away into insignificance. Once again the Church, in the midst of all her weakness and my own, had brought Him to me. And this Mass and this Communion captured the whole mission of the Church — a mission that goes on unceasingly day after day.

Long ago the prophet Malachi foretold "For from the rising of the sun, even to its setting, my name is great among the nations; and everywhere they bring sacrifice to my name, and a pure offering" (Mal 1:11). Every hour of the day in some part of the world a priest, whether in the simplest hut or most magnificent cathedral, on a battlefield or in a prison or refugee camp, is offering Jesus to the Father and to the world and is crying out with John the Baptist "Behold, the Lamb of God, who takes away the sin of the world" (Jn 1:29). He's bringing Jesus to all who come with hunger in their hearts for the Bread of Life. No matter who the priest is, no matter what his limitations, *he is communicating Christ* and what he is doing is representative of the whole mission and work of the priesthood and the entire Catholic Church.

When I preach or counsel or celebrate sacraments, I'm very conscious now of helping everyone to encounter and experience Jesus Christ and welcome Him more fully into their lives. I know, however, it was not always that way. For that I want to ask you to forgive me, to forgive any of us priests or members of the Church who have failed you — failed to convey very simply what is meant to be the purpose of it all — to show the beautiful face of Jesus Christ by our words and our actions. Certainly what we are all about is Jesus Christ —but do we say it enough? Do we show it enough? Do we mean it enough? Do all of us priests and leaders have enough of a deep personal relationship with Him to be able to convey it to others? Do we foster that relationship day by day in our lives by prayer, by the Scriptures, and by all that we do?

At the beginning of the Second Vatican Council, the assembled fathers expressed their purpose: "We as pastors devote all our energies and thoughts to the renewal of ourselves and the flocks committed to us, so that there may radiate before all men the lovable features of Jesus Christ . . . " [1] For the times those features have been blurred and obscured by our sins and shortcomings, please forgive us. Just as we need to ask and give forgiveness to one another all along the way, so also we need to forgive our priests, our bishops, our professed religious, our fellow parishioners. We need reconciliation with all our brothers and sisters in the family of the Church.

Thank God we have a Pope who teaches us the way of forgiveness as he even visits and embraces his attempted assassin in his prison cell. Thank God too that we have a spiritual leader who lives and expresses so clearly the ever old and ever new mission of the Church. Standing on the balcony of St. Peter's, shortly after he was elected, he announced to the whole world that with Peter, the first Pope, he was committed to carrying on the mission of boldly proclaiming everywhere Jesus Christ as *"the Messiah, the Son of the living God"* (Mt 16:16).

Chapter 4

PUTTING FLESH ON
HIS FORGIVENESS

"Why the Church? I can tell my sins to God!"

A lady once told me this story about herself. She had stopped going to confession. She used to say to herself, "'I don't need to go to confession; I can just tell my sins to God'. Then one day when I was telling my sins to God," she said, "God told me, 'I want you to go to confession!', and God gave me a reason. He said, 'I want you to go to confession because *I want to put flesh on my forgiveness!*'"

What a profound expression of the whole plan of salvation in our Lord Jesus Christ *and His Church!* God didn't have to do it that way. He didn't have to be born in a stable, grow up in an insignificant village, work by the sweat of His brow, walk the dusty roads of our earth, be contradicted, have nails driven into His hands and feet, and die on a cross. But that's His way. He wanted to make His love visible, take our flesh and meet us on our own level in a visible, tangible way. And when He finished His earthly work and left us in that earthly, fleshy, visible way, He left among us a visible, earthly, fleshy Church and in that Church visible tangible sacred signs (sacraments) through which He continues His sanctifying and unifying work among us. One of these signs is the sacrament of reconciliation.

"But no man can forgive sins!" Do you know they said that about Jesus too? In three of the Gospel narratives we find that incident in which Jesus tells the paralytic, "Your sins are forgiven you" — and people accused Him of blasphemy, adding, "Who but God alone can forgive sins?" (Mt 9:3, Mk 2:7, Lk 5:21).

They said it of Jesus because they only saw a man. They failed to recognize God in Him, working in and through Him. And they do the same with the Church. Only God can forgive offenses against Himself; but just as God in Jesus forgave as he walked among us in the flesh, so Jesus continues to forgive and make that forgiveness visible through His body the Church.

How much clearer can it be? That resurrection evening when He appeared to the disciples, He said, "As the Father sent me, so I send you." Then He breathed on them, as a sign of empowerment, and said, "Receive the Holy Spirit. Whose sins you forgive are forgiven them, and whose sins you retain are retained" (Jn 20:21-23).

But some say, "Well, that refers to baptism or the preaching of repentance." Well, why not say it includes all of these things? But why stop there? It also includes the power given to the Church over sin, including the sins committed after baptism. And that's where the sacrament of reconciliation comes in.

Why are we so sure about that? Ultimately because the Church — guided by the Spirit — has come to understand, teach, and practice this as God's plan for us. Just as He, Jesus, has power over sin ("But that you may know that the Son of man has authority on earth to forgive sins" Mt 9:6), so He has solemnly imparted that power to His Church with the right to determine how it will be exercised. It's Jesus forgiving down the ages through His Church and through those ordained and appointed in the Church for that ministry.

But it is also, in another sense, the Church forgiving. Every sin we commit affects other people. There is no such thing as a purely private sin. That's true even in our thoughts. If I keep pride in my heart or anger or lust, I can't say, "Well, that's my own business." No, I'm hurting other people. I'm connected with all my brothers and sisters, especially those who are members of the Church, the Body of Christ. When I block the flow of God's life in myself, I'm blocking the good that I can contribute to everyone else — the peace, the joy, the love. And when I want to repent of that, especially when it's serious sin, I need not only tell God I'm sorry (God who is ready to forgive me as soon as I turn back to Him from my heart out of love), but also to tell the Church I'm sorry. Yet I don't have to stand up on Sunday morning and tell my sins to the whole congregation. When I go to the priest, the one ordained and appointed in the Church for that ministry, and when he forgives me as a father or as a big brother in that family of the Church, it's like the whole Church putting their arms around me and saying, "And we forgive you, too; you're also reconciled with us, your family, the Church."

A lot of people outside the Catholic Church seem to have a greater appreciation of the value of confession than many Catholics. I've had persons who are not Catholic come to me just because they wanted to tell their sins to someone who would hear and respond to them in a tangible way. Look at Alcoholics Anonymous. One of the twelve steps towards recovery is that you not only make a thorough inventory of your failings and sins, but that you also find another human being and in great detail admit to that person the wrongs that you have done. AA works with people all over the world of different faiths and of no faith, but they know that it is part of the healing process for all of us that you not only admit your sins to yourself, and to a "higher power", but that you also admit them to another human being.

The little but powerful book on building Christian community called Life Together, by the great Lutheran theologian Dietrich Bonhoeffer (who lived and died heroically under Hitler's persecution) talks about the value of confession to one another. He says, "Sin wants to remain unknown. It shuns the light. In the darkness of the unexpressed it poisons the whole being of a person. This can happen even in the midst of a pious community. *In confession the light of the Gospel breaks into the darkness and seclusion of the heart.* The sin must be brought into the light. The unexpressed must be openly spoken and acknowledged. All that is secret and hidden is made manifest. It is a hard struggle until the sin is openly admitted. But God breaks gates of brass and bars of iron (Ps 107:16)." [1]

Another Protestant minister, Earl Jabay, has written an entire book on the subject of confession and spiritual direction. He recommends to everyone a monthly meeting with another person for the purpose of sharing honestly what you're doing with your time, your talents, your money— everything—to let Jesus be the Lord of it all. And he urges confession of sins to that person. He says, "We Protestants have not had the grace to admit that *we have made a serious mistake in abandoning the confessional at the time of the Reformation.* Our Roman Catholic brethren have since corrected whatever problems there were with the confessional. It is now time for Protestants to return to the discipline of the confessional. Let the confessional first be established among Protestants and later, perhaps, this may serve as part of the bridge which will end our unhappy division." 2

Jabay, Bonhoeffer, and AA all affirm the value of the confession of sins not only to God but to another brother or sister in His family but they do not necessarily regard this as a sacrament of the Church.

For us Catholics, however, confession is not just a good or even important practice. We believe that Jesus did give a special commission and empowerment to His Church over the reign of sin and Satan, and that through the repentant confession of sins to a priest and the words of forgiveness, Jesus is acting in a very unique way to break the chains of sin, overcome the powers of darkness, and grace us on our way. "As the Father has sent me, so I send you . . . Receive the holy Spirit. Whose sins you forgive are forgiven them, . . ." (Jn 20:21-23).

Some people say, however, that they have gone to confession many, many times but they see little change in their lives. Maybe they don't earnestly enough want or expect any change through the power of God and their own cooperation. Maybe they're failing to bring to the sacrament what really has to be brought. I've had the experience (rarely!) of someone who is forty or fifty years of age saying in confession "I disobeyed my Momma!" The person probably always said that ever since his first confession. The nuns had said that's something you can say in confession, so he's been saying it ever since. Confession had become, possibly, just a routine.

When we go to confession we need to look at our real lives — married or single, type of work or lack of work, neighborhood, parish or community involvements—and confess honestly what we're doing or not doing with our lives right now. Then we need to go a step further and ask, "What is the main thing that keeps hanging me up, the predominant fault, the main underlying failing in my life?"

We used to talk about the seven root or capital sins. Do you remember them? They're pride, covetousness, lust, anger, gluttony, envy, and laziness. (I recall the first time I ever heard someone explain those capital sins. I was sitting out there in the pews, and I thought to myself, "Wow, I've got all of 'em!") I guess we, or most of us, struggle with all of them but there is usually one that is our predominant struggle. If it's not one of those it may be some variation of one of them. In any case, after we have told our sins as we know them (especially any serious ones) it would be very helpful to add, "and this is what I think is the main thing that needs to change in my life."

Together with the desire and decision for real change and conversion (turning away from sin and turning towards God, the source of grace and new life) we should confess with true contrition. On one priests' retreat, the director asked us all: "When was the last time you shed a tear for your sins?" As I thought about it, I couldn't remember *ever* shedding tears because of my sins (except when my Dad would put me over his knee and wallop my backside!). I know, of course, that you don't have to cry to be truly sorry.

But since that retreat and that question, I have shed some tears (not nearly enough!); and I know now that if there is anything I should ever shed a tear about, it is that I have offended You, my God, who are **all good** and *deserving of all my love.*

Whereas many prepare inadequately for the sacrament, not earnestly asking the Holy Spirit to enlighten them and give them true contrition and conversion, there are others, however, who go through too much before confession, almost working themselves up into a cold sweat. If you honestly can think of no particular sins, you can still make a good confession by simply saying to the priest, "I can't think of anything specific right now, but I know I'm a sinner and I'm sorry and repent of all the sins of my life." (In fact, it's good to conclude every confession with this expression of sorrow for all past sins.)

There are others too who worry, "Suppose I get nervous and miss something or don't say it right!" I still remember the retreat master from high school days who said: "Can you picture Mary Magdalene running behind Our Lord asking 'Hey Jesus, are you sure you got it right about that night in Tiberias?" She came to Jesus and went away a new woman. We too encounter Him in this wonderful sacrament and are meant to go away renewed and at peace. It's not primarily what we do but what *He* does. Our part is to be honest and repentant. Don't deliberately conceal anything serious (which could make it a useless and bad confession); but even if you *forget* a hundred things in a sincere confession, they are all forgiven. If it is something truly grave that you forgot, tell it in the next confession whenever that is. In the meantime, be at peace and feel free to receive Holy

Communion. Remember too, you can always say to the priest very simply, "Father, I'm nervous. Help me make a good confession."

Every good confession is a humbling of our pride, an experience of the cross, a dying to self. It is also, however, a door to that peace that the world can never give. (Jn 14:27). That first Easter night when Jesus commissioned His Church to forgive sins, His words were first of all, "Peace be with you." The sacrament is meant to be one, not of fear, but of peace and joy.

I remember the first time I heard confessions for a whole class of little children who were preparing for their first Holy Communion. I walked into the classroom and told the children, "We're going over now for your first confession" — and they all applauded! I don't know what the teacher had told them in preparation for confession; but whatever she did, she did a great job. Those little children didn't look to confession with dread or nervousness, but with joy. She must have said something like, "Jesus loves you and He died on the cross and rose again so that you could live a whole new life. In this sacrament, it's Jesus, through the priest, who forgives your sins. You can tell Him anything. He'll understand and forgive you, and you'll be new and clean and happy and able to love God and others more."

It is true that some people have had bad experiences with confession — sometimes even as children. Something connected with confession hurt or frightened them and the memory still causes trouble when they approach the sacrament now. Like every bad or fearful memory, however, this can be healed. If forgiveness is called for, give it "from (your) heart" (Mt 18:35) to the priest, teacher, parent or whomever. Just wanting to forgive is the main thing. Open your heart to Jesus and ask Him who loves and is ready to forgive that person, to do it in and through you. You could also invite Jesus back into that memory when the incident occurred, and without forcing it, picture Him with you at the time it happened. Rest in that for awhile, letting Jesus minister and speak to you in the quiet of your heart, asking Him calmly to heal. Remember it is He who is always the chief invisible minister of the sacrament; and the priest, like the Church herself, is but His very limited human instrument.

There are those who go to confession, but there may be something serious in the back of their minds that they have never had the courage to confess. They're embarrassed, ashamed, and they wonder what the priest would think of them. Let me tell you what I would think of you — and I know enough about my brother priests to know that what I think is the way, at least in general, that they would think and feel as well.

When someone comes to confession who is carrying a heavy burden of sin — maybe something that has always seemed much too embarrassing to confess — and then finally gets it out, you know the way I feel? It's one of the happiest times in my life as a priest. That's why I became a priest! It's like being a doctor. You don't go through all that training just to put band-aids on people. When someone comes along who is really hurting and you're able to help that person in a significant way — you feel it's worth it all.

And if I met that person afterwards, what would I think? First of all, I might not even connect the person with the confession. In most confessionals you have an option. You can either go face to face or you can go anonymously behind a screen. (You could even in extreme embarrassment write your sins, hand the paper to the priest, and say you're sorry for these and all the sins of your life.) In any case, we priests don't go around every day thinking of the things we've heard in confession! By and large, they get lost in the shuffle. But even if I would remember it and know the person, how would I feel in that person's presence? I would feel so much respect for that person's honesty and courage. I would feel a special reverence in the company of that person and a greater bond of closeness and love. I would feel very humble and have a deep sense of gratitude to God for what happened that day when that burden was laid down and God's grace broke through in such a wonderful way!

Resist the temptation to hold back anything serious in confession — or even to "pretty up" your sins. The simpler you say it the better. The fullness of the joy and peace that often accompany this sacrament has a lot to do with the quality of the confession.

We Catholics are encouraged to confess our sins to God in the privacy of our own hearts at the beginning of every Mass and even every night before going to sleep. But we are also ordinarily required by Church law to confess to a priest *(if guilty of serious sin)* once a year or before Holy Communion. More frequent confession is the ideal and is strongly recommended by the Church. We priests are expected to go to confession regularly ourselves to another priest. Having tried to practice that myself with spiritual direction on a monthly basis throughout the years of my priesthood, *I can testify to the incalculable value of it.*

As I go around giving parish mission renewals and retreats, I can also testify that some of the best things that happen during them are the things that happen in the sacred secrecy of the confessional or reconciliation room. They are known only to God and the individuals involved. There are many good people who neglect the sacrament for long periods of time saying, "I don't need to go." When they finally come, however, and admit their sinfulness humbly and honestly to the Church, and receive absolution — what chains are broken, what doors are opened and how much healing and new life breaks through!

In the light of this experience I can understand better the repeated call of John Paul II, beginning with his first encyclical letter, for a new appreciation and frequent use of this sacrament. Always working for genuine renewal in the light of the true spirit of Vatican II, he writes that some today "are inclined to replace exaggerated attitudes of the past with other exaggerations: from seeing sin everywhere they pass to not recognizing it anywhere; from too much emphasis on the fear of eternal punishment they pass to preaching a love of God that excludes any punishment deserved by sin." 3 It is also understandable why an entire synod of representatives of the bishops of the world would devote itself in 1983 to the subject and sacrament of reconciliation. (The Pope's remarks just quoted were part of his sharing the fruits of this Synod.)

All this underlines the request of Our Lady of Fatima relating to monthly confession (in connection with the five first Saturdays devotion) and the numerous reported messages from Medjugorje encouraging regular confession as part of our ongoing conversion. In fact, one of these earlier messages of August 6, 1982 is, "One must invite people to go to confession each month, especially the first Saturday . . . Monthly confessions will be a remedy for the Church in the West." 4

The "intellectual" problems many have with the Church, her teachings and confession are often rooted in personal moral problems. The Church is contradicting or challenging their way of life. A humble, repentant use of the sacrament of reconciliation opens the door to a whole new relationship not only with God but with the Church as well. Bishop Fulton Sheen told the story of the Catholic who came to him with a list of intellectual objections to the Church. The Bishop said he'd be glad to talk about all of them but first suggested that the person go to confession. After the initial shock and resistance to the idea, the person confessed. "Now", the Bishop said, "let's talk about your objections." "I don't have them anymore" was the reply.

There is a passage in the 2nd book of Kings, Chapter 5 about Naaman, the army commander of the Arameans, who was a leper. An Israelite slave girl captured by the Arameans tells him that there is a prophet in her country who can heal him. Naaman receives a letter from his own master, the king of Aram, to the king of Israel and sets out with his retinue and many gifts to find the healer. When finally he arrives with all his horses and chariots at the door of Elisha's house, he is told by the prophet, "Go wash seven times in the Jordan and your flesh will heal, and you will be clean." Naaman's pride is insulted and he's livid with rage! "I thought that he would surely come out and stand there to invoke the Lord his God, and would move his hand over the spot, and thus cure the leprosy. Are not the rivers of Damascus the Abana and the Pharpar, better than all the waters of Israel? Could I not wash in them and be cleansed?" And he turned away in anger and left. But his servants came up and reasoned with him. "My father," they said, "If the prophet had told you to do something extraordinary, would you not have done it? All the more now since he said to you 'wash and be clean,' should you do as he said. So Naaman went down and plunged into the Jordan seven times at the word of the man of God. **His flesh became again like the flesh of a little child, and he was cured.**"(vv. 1-14)

Like Naaman we have our own ideas of how God should help and heal us; and we're often looking for the unusual and extraordinary and miss what's right under our noses. But God says, "Just do what my Son Jesus and His Church tell you." The seven washings in the river Jordan could be for us a symbol of the seven sacraments of Jesus and His Church. *Through the proper use of these simple external signs of Christ and His Church, we plunge ever more deeply into the mystery of His death and resurrection and continue to be made clean and new and whole.*

GIFT OF THE CHURCH

Chapter 5

HOW CAN I KNOW
THE TRUTH?

"But it's not in the Bible!"

"For this I was born and for this I came into the world, to testify to the truth. Everyone who belongs to the truth listens to my voice," Jesus says as He stands before the Roman governor. And Pilate sneers, "What is truth?" (Jn 18:37-38) The role of the Church left us by Jesus Christ is to proclaim the truth — not scientific truth, not psychological truth — but religious truth, the truth about God and our relationship with Him and all that follows from that.

But do we really need the Church? Why can't each person just figure out for himself or herself what to believe and what to do for salvation? If that were the case, then it would never have been necessary for Jesus Christ to teach anything. He said, however, "For this I was born, for this I came into the world, to testify to the truth" (Jn 18:37). Beyond that, it certainly wouldn't have been necessary for Him to send out His Church, "Go, therefore, and make disciples of all nations. . .teaching them to observe all that I have commanded you" (Mt 28:19-20).

What about the Bible, though, isn't that sufficient? Undoubtedly the Bible is a source of religious truth. All the different Christian denominations, however, make use of the Bible — and yet, there are still so many denominations, thousands of them, — and new ones continue to spring up! Different denominations derive different and even contradictory meanings from the same book. If there is no authority outside of the Bible to interpret what's in the Bible, we're still left without a true guide in matters of faith.

Just as the Constitution needs the Supreme Court to interpret it, so the Bible needs the Church. There is a difference however. The Supreme Court is *merely* human and can make disastrous mistakes like Roe vs. Wade. The Church on the other hand is uniquely guided by the same Holy Spirit who inspired the authors of the Bible.

Even the decision as to what books belong to the Bible could not possibly come from the Bible itself. It was up to an authority other than the Bible to make that decision. That authority was the Church — the Catholic Church. Historically, the Church began before the New Testament of the Bible. If it had not been for the Church, there would be no Christian Bible; and without the Church to interpret it, the Bible remains an inadequate guide to faith. 1

Jesus never wrote anything of which we have a record; nor is there any evidence in His lifetime that He instructed anyone to write in His name. What He did, however, was to teach by word and action; and He clearly commissioned His disciples to go to the ends of the earth and teach, promising to be with them always in carrying out that mission (Mt 28:19-20). What they taught and preached, and what the Church believed and practiced under the guidance of these first apostles and their disciples, is what we call Apostolic Tradition, the lived faith of the Church in the apostolic age.

Little by little, in various places and at various times, some of this teaching was committed to writing and some of these writings were eventually discerned and selected by the Church as the inspired books of the New Testament.

Long before this happened, however, the Church was in existence - preaching, teaching, baptizing, offering the Eucharist, serving the needs of the people. None of the books of the New Testament were written until about 50 A.D., a number of years after Our Lord's ascension, and the composition of the last book (2 Peter) seems to extend even into the 2nd century. Before all these books were compiled to form the New Testament of the Bible as we have it today, nearly two and a half centuries had passed! The final determination as to exactly what books belonged to the Bible was made by the Church. Among the earliest official decisions about this were those of Pope Damasus and the provincial councils of Hippo and Carthage in the late 4th century and, then finally, at the general council of Trent in the 1500s.

The books of the Bible are regarded by the Catholic Church as the **inspired Word of God**, and Church teachings never contradict it and are reflected in it. But even the Bible itself nowhere says that it contains everything that has been revealed by God. When somebody says, *"But, it's got to be in the Bible!" I like to ask, "Who says so?" Did Jesus ever say that? Does even the Bible say that? Where in the Bible does it say, "It's got to be in the Bible"?*

Actually, what was written in the New Testament was what was being preached and taught and lived by the Church before it was ever written down. Scripture then is a crystallization in writing of the tradition. As Paul puts it, "I handed on to you as of first importance what I also received . . ." (1Cor 15:3). Paul received the tradition, handed it on, and is now committing it to writing. Elsewhere he says, "Therefore, brothers, stand firm and hold fast to the traditions that you were taught, either by an oral statement or by a letter of ours" (2 Thes 2:15). That not all of the tradition was written down is testified to by the Apostle John himself at the end of his Gospel when he says, "There are also many other things that Jesus did, but if these things were to be described individually, I do not think the whole world would contain the books that would be written." The Scriptures then contain only a reflection of what was being taught and lived by the Church before it was put down in writing. And even what was written can only be understood correctly in the context of what was being taught and lived by the Church at the time it was written.

To know then the fullness of what God has revealed to us through Jesus and the apostles guided by the Spirit, we need to pay attention not only to the written word in the Scriptures but also to tradition. Tradition, from the Latin *traditio*, means something handed down. All that was handed down from very ancient times in the life of the Church can be gathered not just from Scripture but also from the writings of early Church Fathers; ancient inscriptions and images (such as those in the catacombs); hymns and poems; and other historical evidences of teachings and beliefs, practices, and ways of worship. These are sources of tradition. As the Second Vatican Council expresses it, "The

Church, in her teaching, life and worship, perpetuates and hands onto all generations all that she herself is, all that she believes." 2 Among the witnesses of the tradition are especially the writings of the Fathers of the Church. If we want to know how the early Christians believed and lived and worshiped, how they understood the message of Jesus and His apostles and interpreted the Scriptures — we need to be in touch with these early Church writers. For example, take Ignatius of Antioch, third successor of St. Peter as Bishop of that city and a man who had personally heard the Apostle John. Ignatius suffered death for his Christian faith by wild beasts in the Roman Ampitheater about the year 110. On his way to martyrdom, he wrote seven letters to various Christian communities to strengthen them in the faith, to uphold true doctrine and to encourage unity, genuine active charity and faithful obedience to legitimate authority, especially to their bishops. In these letters, Ignatius strongly affirms the humanity and divinity of Jesus Christ ("God in man, true life in death, both of Mary and from God"), 3 the bodily virginity of Mary, the mysterious but real bodily presence of Jesus in the Holy Eucharist, the ecclesiastical orders of bishop, priest and deacon — and more. In fact, according to John Henry Newman, great English convert to the Catholic Church and scholar of the Fathers, all Catholic doctrine in outline is contained, in the letters of Ignatius.

To see what the Fathers have to say on many different teachings of the Church I would recommend William Jurgens' book The Faith of the Early Fathers. 4 It's been an invaluable source for me, that has an unusual doctrinal index, referencing significant passages from their writings covering subjects like the Trinity, the Incarnation, the

Church, Mary, the Pope, the Mass and the seven sacraments, original sin, the Christian life and purgatory.

A couple of years ago I met a young doctor who had been a member of a Pentecostal denomination. He told me that he became a Catholic chiefly because of reading the early Fathers. As a Pentecostal he had a personal relationship with Jesus, was open to the Holy Spirit and knew the Bible but he had begun to see the great need for correct doctrine. As he read the Fathers, he realized that the Catholic Church went back 2000 years and that the Holy Spirit had been with the Church all along and that he needed the guidance of that Church to know fully what God wanted him to believe and do for salvation.

Church tradition, however, is not a static thing but, under the guidance of the Holy Spirit, a living and growing reality. "This tradition which comes from the apostles develops in the Church with the help of the Holy Spirit. For there is a growth in the understanding of the realities and the words which have been handed down." (Vat.II)5 This is true of the Scriptures themselves. The Gospels (especially of Matthew and John) and the Epistles (particularly those of Paul) already show how deeper insights into the original teaching are beginning to emerge and *theologies* (ways of expressing the revelation) are being developed.

Just as an acorn grows into a huge oak tree and a fertilized ovum into a full grown human being, so also the full understanding of all that Jesus and the apostles left us is unfolded only little by little over the ages, through the watering of God's grace and the sunshine of the Holy Spirit. The oak tree is contained in the acorn and the fertilized egg is already a human being (with all his or her DNA), but time is needed for everything to develop and unfold. So, too, in the life of the Church — growth is a sign of life. This continual development in understanding the full implications of the Gospel and of the early teaching and preaching is a sign of dynamic vitality.

Drawing from Scripture and tradition under the direction of the Spirit of Jesus, our ultimate guide to faith is the teaching Church herself — the bishops gathered around the Pope — the successors of the apostles united with Peter, who form the ordinary teaching authority or *magisterium* of Christ's Church.

A good example of how Scripture and tradition can merge is in the doctrine of the Holy Eucharist. Some think that the words of Jesus are clear enough, "This is my body; this is my blood." The same is true of other passages in the Bible about the Eucharist, such as St. Paul's account in which he says "whoever eats the bread or drinks the cup of the Lord unworthily will have to answer for the body and blood of the Lord" (1 Cor 11:23-32) and Jesus' discourse about Himself as "the bread of life" where He says, "For my flesh is true food, and my blood is true drink" (Jn 6:41-58). But many interpret these texts in a symbolic way, and the argument and division between Christians goes on and on.

How is the Catholic Church so sure about her position? Well, it's based on Scripture — but *not* on Scripture alone. It's based also on what was being preached, believed, and practiced by Christians before being written down in the Bible and on the constant belief and practice of the Church down through the ages.

We know from very early Christian witnesses and writers that the followers of Christ really believed that the bread and wine, after the consecration, were no longer merely bread and wine, but that they were the Body and

Blood of the Lord — not just symbolically, but truly. This witness, this tradition, is a source of faith just like the Bible.

Martin Luther himself, who is identified with the "sola Scriptura" or Scripture alone position, made this statement about the real presence of Christ in the Eucharist: "This article has been harmoniously believed throughout the world to this hour; from the wisdom of our fathers' books and scripts, both in Greek and in Latin ... for it is frightening and shocking to hear or to believe anything that is contrary to the harmonious testimony, beliefs, and teachings of the Holy Christian Church as passed on from its beginning through 1500 years and held as the truth throughout the whole world." He goes on to say about those who hold the opposite, "Their own opinion (the rotten ghosts) professes against them for they argue about the text and quarrel with each other, there are seven or eight different versions." Luther considered the words of Scripture to be clear enough on the subject, but he recognizes the great confusion among those who are relying on Scripture alone, and he appeals to tradition. In fact, in the context of this letter, he says that on this matter tradition alone should be sufficient. [6]

Even the inspiration of the Scriptures themselves is something I accept ultimately because the Church teaches it — based on tradition! The Scriptures can't prove their own inspiration. There were many writings circulated in the early days of Christianity about Our Lord and His life and teachings. The Christian community had to discern which ones were in accord with the beliefs and practices handed down in the Church and were divinely inspired. This understanding emerged gradually and became something passed on from generation to generation. This tradition was finally officially taught and established by Church Councils.

The Catholic Church teaches from both Scripture and tradition. But the Church herself is the teacher given us by Jesus: "Go, therefore, and make disciples ... teaching them ..." (Mt 28:19-20) — guiding us, in the Spirit, to all truth. "The Church of the living God," the Bible says, "is the pillar and foundation of truth" (1 Tim 3:15). "As the Father has sent me, so I send you" (Jn 20:21), Jesus said to the leaders of his Church. Without the Church, what other sure guide do we have?

A.A. Curtis, D.D., who had been rector of Mt. Calvary Protestant Episcopal Church in Baltimore and who became the Catholic Bishop of Wilmington, wrote these words before embracing the Catholic Church: "I am tired to death of uncertainty. I am sick of self-will. I am weary of standing alone . . . I must find a living, speaking, infallible authority to which to submit, or else I must disregard Christianity as a miserable sham . . . I have determined to go abroad for awhile and to make there my submission to the Chair of Peter, if after consulting with some whom I have promised to consult, my mind is still to the effect that Anglicanism is spurious and that the Roman obedience is alone entitled to my allegiance." [7]

"You will know the truth," Jesus said, "and the truth will set you free" (Jn 8:32). But how will we know the truth about God and the things we are to believe and do in His regard? Paul addresses that when he says: "But how can they call on him in whom they have not believed? And how can they believe in him of whom they have not heard? And how can they hear without someone to preach? And how can people preach unless they are sent?" (Rom 10:14-15). Jesus sent out His apostles to the ends of the earth to preach and teach. "Go, therefore, and make disciples of all the nations, baptizing them in the name of the Father, and of the Son, and of the Holy Spirit, teaching them to observe all that I have commanded you. And behold, I am with you always, until the end of the age" (Mt 28: 19-20). This is the way—through a living, teaching Church, one that goes back to Him in history and one that still relies on His promise: "I am with you always."

Before the end of the first century, St. Clement, Bishop of Rome and successor of St. Peter, writes to the Christians of Corinth urging them to heal a schism in their local Church and accept the authority of the legitimate successors of the Apostles. He says, "The Apostles received the Gospel for us from the Lord Jesus Christ; and Jesus Christ was sent from God. Christ, therefore, is from God, and the Apostles are from Christ....Through countryside and city they preached; and they appointed their earliest converts, testing them by the Spirit, to be bishops and deacons of future believers." 8

Irenaeus, another Father of the Church and second bishop of Lyons, in his great work Against Heresies written about the year 185, lists the bishops of Rome from the time of Peter and Paul and says, "In this order, and by the teaching of the Apostles handed down in the Church, the preaching of the truth has come down to us". 9 "When, therefore, we have such proofs, *it is not necessary to seek among others the truth which is easily obtained from the Church.* For the Apostles, like a rich man in a bank, deposited with her most copiously everything which pertains to the truth; and everyone whosoever wishes draws from her the drink of life . . . What then? If there should be a dispute over some kind of question, ought we not have recourse to the most ancient Churches in which the Apostles were familiar, and draw from them what is clear and certain in regard to that question?" [10]

As Jesus was sent from the Father, Jesus sent the Church. As we accept Him, we accept His Church; as we believe Him, we believe His Church.

The Church is usually dealing with supernatural realities. She is dealing in mystery. When we begin to pick and choose what we're going to believe, where do we begin and where do we end? The Trinity, the Incarnation, redemption, sanctification, the Holy Eucharist, eternal life — they are all mysteries. Every one of those realities (which also influence moral teachings) is beyond full human comprehension. We accept them because God revealed them and His Church proclaims them. The work of theology is to help put the mystery in human terms. It is a servant of the faith. When it begins to explain away the mystery, like some theologians do, it's no longer a servant but a destroyer of the faith. It has gone beyond its purpose.

When it comes to mysteries of our faith, if I accept any of them, I should accept all of them. The reason is the only ultimately secure basis for accepting any is the basis that God has revealed and His Church proclaims. The same is true of the authoritative long-standing moral teachings of the Church. The Church has always understood that they too are part and parcel of her mission, as stated by the Second Vatican Council and included in Jesus' commission to His Church to teach "all that I have commanded you" (Mt 28:20).

We should be able to know moral truths just from reason and conscience, but our reason is often clouded by our own passions, prejudices and sinfulness, therefore God, in His mercy, has come to our aid by revealing the moral law as we find it contained explicitly or implicitly in Scripture and tradition. From these sources — natural reason and divine revelation — the Church teaches morality in His name. As Vatican II expresses it: *"In the formation of their consciences, the Christian faithful ought carefully to attend to the sacred and certain doctrine of the Church. The Church is, by the will of Christ, the teacher of the truth. It is her duty to give utterance to and authoritatively to teach that Truth which is Christ Himself, and also to declare and confirm by her authority those principles of the moral order which have their origin in human nature itself."* [11] That the Council Fathers understood that the Church's authority (like Scripture) encompasses very specific moral issues and judgments is evident from those Conciliar passages where they speak out in no uncertain terms against particular human actions as immoral e.g. abortion, euthanasia, mutilation, prostitution, physical or mental torture, whatever insults human dignity, [12] blameworthy methods of birth regulation, [13] indiscriminate war-time bombing, etc. [14]

When we ourselves choose what we're going to follow among the Church's moral teachings, where do we start and stop? Are we not doing our own thing instead of His, following our own way instead of the way of the Lord?

* * * * *

I remember an experience in Malaysia where a number of years ago I had been invited to teach and preach over a period of six weeks. For the first time in my life, I found myself living in a non-Christian country. In some of the villages there were still witch-doctors and in the cities Buddhist and Hindu temples which I visited. Buddhists do not necessarily believe in God, and Hindus may believe in many gods; and the country was controlled by Muslims who do not believe in Jesus Christ as the divine Son of God. At the time I was also studying the origin of the various Christian denominations — how one after the other broke off from the Catholic Church or from those who had already broken from this Mother Church, contradicting one another and often continuing to split up among themselves. I was also reading the history of one of the Councils of the Church and the all-too-human politicizing involved in it. With all of this twirling around in my head, I remember one night getting out of bed in almost a cold sweat, bombarded with attacks on my own beliefs.

Sitting down at the desk in my room, I wrote in a day-book from deep in my guts what I believe about God our Father, about Jesus his Son, my Brother, Savior and Lord, about the Holy Spirit, about the Church which He gave us to guide us down through the ages, about the Holy Eucharist and Mary and on down the line. As I remember it, it was the words of Peter on the occasion of Jesus' discourse about Himself as "the bread of life" from the sixth chapter of John's Gospel that popped into my mind. When Jesus concluded His sermon, many of His disciples turned away and "no longer accompanied Him" saying, "This saying is hard; who can accept it?" Jesus didn't try to call them back but turned to His apostles and asked, "Do you also want to leave?" Peter answered, "Master, to whom shall we go? You have the words of eternal life" (Jn 6:60-68). That night I made those words of Peter my own: *"Lord, if I left that Mother Church, where else could I go for truth? You and Your Church have the words of everlasting life."*

When I arrived back in the U.S., it was Lent and I had a schedule of one mission after the other, with the last one during Holy Week in the little town of Violet, south of New Orleans. At the Easter Vigil service I was asked by the pastor to be the one to carry the Easter candle up the aisle in the darkened Church and to sing three times the refrain "Christ Our Light". I remember the chills that ran down my spine as the candle was lit and I began that walk in the darkened church. In Malaysia, I had experienced what the world would be like (and what I would be like!) without the Light of Jesus Christ — the darkness of those who do not know God as revealed by Jesus and the confusion of those who no longer accept his Church. How proudly, yet with such humble gratitude and joy, I bellowed out those words —"Christ Our Light"!

It was a proclamation that *He truly is the "light of the world" (Jn 8:12) and that his Church has the mission of keeping that light (of his truth and message) pure and undimmed, bearing it to the ends of the earth and letting it illumine every aspect of human life!*

Chapter 6

THE CATHOLIC CHURCH
AND UNITY

"That the world may believe!" (Jn 17:21)

At the last supper, according to John's Gospel, the Savior pours out His heart in prayer for unity: "I pray not only for them, but also for those who will believe in me through their word, so *that they may all be one*, as you, Father, are in me and I in you, that they also may be in us, *that the world may believe that you sent me"* (Jn 17:20-21). That is the great miracle He prayed for before He died — not that mountains would move or stars fall from heaven but that His followers would be joined in unity and love! *That's the miracle by which the world will believe!* How far (it seems) are we from that goal right now!

It's not just a question of the divisions among all the various Christian denominations, but the divisions in the Catholic Church as well. True it is that we have the basic structure for unity more than any other Christian denomination and many evidences of a remarkable unity of discipline, doctrine, and worship. But there are also glaring and disturbing signs of disunity among us Catholics. Once again in the newspaper there is an article (at the time of this writing) about a large number of theologians who say they have no duty to follow the Pope in the appointment of certain bishops or when he teaches on such moral issues as contraception, homosexuality and divorce. There is also presently in the news the story of the break away from the authority of the bishop of certain parishes or congregations that are no longer willing to obey his directives. And the news items go on and on.

It's nice to dream about unity. It's tough to bring it about. That's true in marriage; it's true in family life; it's true in any community. It's true in the Church. It takes a lot of soul-searching, forgiving, humility, sacrifice, and love. It takes no less than the dying to self so that something new can be born. What is new in marriage is that people are no longer two but one flesh; what is new in the family or community is that there is a family and not just a house full of individuals; and what is new in the Church is that we are no longer disjointed bones and pieces of flesh, but we are one body in Christ.

The Holy Spirit is the source of that unity, and the Holy Spirit has enlightened and guided us about a very down-to-earth and concrete way of bringing that unity about. The recognition of one head in the Church, one visible head under Jesus the invisible Head, and one chief shepherd in each part of the Church, the bishop, in union with the chief bishop, the successor of Peter is God's plan for the unity of His Church. It's so simple, but it's tough to carry out. Everybody who has ever tried to carry it out has his or her own story to tell, and it includes not "doing your own thing".

I've had my own rebellions and struggles with Church authority, but as I also reflect on my experience of obedience, I can see the hand of God at work in it. Every regular assignment I have ever had, until the present one, was something I would never have asked for myself. I grew up in the uptown area of New Orleans (and uptown/downtown are two different worlds), but my first regular assignment was to a downtown parish, followed by another that was even farther downtown. I was a city kid and wasn't familiar with outlying or country areas, but guess where I was sent for my first pastorate! After nine years as a country pastor, I had a plan for doing full time parish mission work and retreat work, etc., when the bishop called me in to take an inner city, predominantly black parish. None of these parish assignments would I have picked on my own, but as I look back on them, I can see that God had His hand in it all (through the bishop). One sign of this is what these appointments did for me. I trust they also did good for others. I know they did good for me. They stretched and broadened me in a way that I personally would not have chosen.

Before I was ever ordained a priest, I had become very interested in socio-economic issues that affected people's lives and was a great enthusiast of the social encyclicals of the Popes. One summer before ordination to the priesthood, I had planned to go up to Notre Dame University to take a course in economics, but trouble with my eyes at the time prevented me. Right after ordination, however, I asked the Archbishop of New Orleans for permission to go off for a while to study economics. He told me, "No."

That was hard to swallow! As I look back, however, I thank God for the bishop's "No." The last thing I needed at that time of my life was to go somewhere and study. My seminary training (especially in those days) had been so theoretical and "ivory tower" that what I really needed was a good big dose of down-to-earth people and day-to-day ministry as a parish priest. The twelve years in a very earthy, average-income parish, plus two in a similar one, afforded me just that, before my appointment as pastor.

But all of this is just to make a simple point. If at any of those times I had refused to go along with the bishop's wishes, I would have missed what God (unknown to me) had in store; and if I had rebelled and gone out on my own, I would have strictly been on my own and no longer a unifying part of the Catholic family.

I believe that whenever we act to build up the unity of the Church, we're doing God's work, the work of the Spirit; and when we do the opposite, we're doing Satan's work, the work of the one who wants to "divide and conquer". *The world needs more than ever the light and guidance of the Church, but the preoccupation with in-fighting and divisions often saps her attention and strength and hinders her witness and mission.* Paul urges us in the fourth chapter of his Letter to the Ephesians, *"Make every effort to preserve the unity which has the Spirit as its origin and peace as its binding force"* (Eph. 4:3) [N.A.B. unrevised edition].

Early Christians understood this as expressed in the New Testament Acts of the Apostles: "the community of believers was of one heart and mind . . ." (4:32). If there is one theme that runs through the seven letters of Ignatius of Antioch, written to communities of Christians in different cities, on his way to martyrdom about the year 110 A.D., it is the theme of unity. Over and over again, he calls for this unity by way of the recognition of legitimate authority especially the authority of the bishop. "Take care to do all things in harmony with God, the bishop presiding in the place of God and the presbyters (priests) in place of the council of the Apostles . . ." [1] "Let no one do anything of concern to the Church without the bishop." [2] He attributes his repetition of this theme to the promptings of the Holy Spirit, "It was the Spirit who kept preaching these words: 'Do nothing without the bishop, keep your body as the temple of God, love unity, flee from divisions, be imitators of Jesus Christ, as he was imitator of the Father.'" [3]

St. Cyprian, Bishop of Carthage in North Africa, in his treatise on The Unity of the Catholic Church (first edition), about the year 251 A.D., writes this regarding the role of Peter and his successors: "The Lord says to Peter: 'I say to you that you are Peter, and upon this rock I will build my Church, and the gates of hell will not overcome it. And to you I will give the keys of the kingdom of heaven: and whatever things you bind on earth shall be bound also in heaven, and whatever you loose on earth, they shall be loosed also in heaven' (Mt 16:18-19). And again He says to him after His resurrection: 'Feed my sheep' (Jn 21:17). On him He builds the Church, and to him He gives the command to feed the sheep; and although He assigns a like power to all the Apostles, yet He founded a single chair, and He established by His own authority a source and an intrinsic reason for that unity. Indeed, the others were that also which Peter was; but a primacy is given to Peter, whereby it is made clear that there is but one Church and one chair. So too, all are shepherds, and the flock is shown to be one, fed by all the Apostles in single-minded accord. *If someone does not hold fast to this unity of Peter, can he imagine that he still holds the faith? If he desert the chair of Peter upon whom the Church was built, can he still be confident that he is in the Church?"* 4

When we disagree with some (non-doctrinal) policy or practice in the Church, whether decreed by the Pope or bishop, pastor or religious superior or parish leader, there is a way of going about it without breaking Catholic unity and causing bad blood in the whole body of the Church. There have been times that I've expressed personally and directly to bishops, under whom I've worked, objections to policies or ways of doing things. In a number of the situations, I've come to see with the passage of years where his way was the best and I was just missing the mark. But, in any case, it's one thing to disagree; it's another to disrupt or divide.

I remember the night in my first pastorate answering the kitchen telephone when I was trying to grab a bite to eat shortly before a parish council meeting. Ed was on the line. He was the only black member of our parish council and chairman of the Human Relations or Social Involvement Committee. What he was telling me was, "Look, Father, I'm not going to that meeting tonight." "Why, Ed?" I asked. "Well," he said, "I've been going to those meetings now for a long time, and we spend a lot of time talking about all kinds of unimportant things. For example, last meeting we spent two hours discussing what the altar boys were going to wear when they served Mass! Then when they get to me, to the report of my committee, nobody seems to be interested! I'm making my report, and heads are down; people are doodling; nobody's really listening. And yet, I thought that's what it was all about, human relations, how we relate to one another, getting along like brothers and sisters in the

Church and in the community. I've had it! I'm through!"

"Ed," I said, "look, I agree with you. But what good does it do to just tell it to me over the telephone? I want you to go to that meeting tonight and tell the whole group what you said to me."

"Well," he said, "maybe . . ." That night Ed showed up at the parish council meeting and when it came time for his report he said to the council what he had said to me on the phone. That night people stopped their doodling, looked up, and listened! They began to ask questions and make suggestions. And they decided to devote an entire meeting just to human relations, which resulted in some meaningful and concrete actions. Ed became an instrument of unity and healing.

I was just talking to a retired (but still working) Jesuit priest, trained as a sociologist, but assigned to several other tasks, in his long career of service, one of which was pastor of a parish. It struck me when he said that one of the early things he did when he became pastor was to invite the bishop to dinner for the feast of St. Ignatius, asking him to come an hour before to meet the parish staff. At the meeting he asked the bishop very simply to let them all know what he expected of them and wanted them to accomplish in the parish. The bishop told them, and he tried to carry it out - receiving at the end of his tenure a heart-warming episcopal letter of appreciation.

It's a simple story, but how much it's needed in the Church today! Suppose every pastor, religious superior and head of every institution and organization in the diocese would do the same! *All the members of "the household of God" (1 Tim 3:15) have one earthly religious superior — above all the others — and he is the bishop, under the chief bishop, the Pope. To work with him in that spirit of unity, obedience and love is to do the will and fulfill the plan of God for His Church.*

There are also, however, many examples of the opposite. I've recently picked up an article in a Catholic magazine that disagrees with the Pope's appointments of bishops in a number of dioceses around the world and also takes issue with the clamping down on certain theologians; and then the writer goes on to say, "Obviously, I am not interested in picking on any egocentric ecclesiastic who has assumed spiritual powers not granted him by Jesus." The article is written by a priest. I'm incensed! Who does this guy think he is, and what does he hope to accomplish? If the Pope doesn't have the authority and responsibility to appoint bishops and guard the faith of the Church — who does? Certainly he's not above criticism; he's human like the rest of us. But if he were egocentric, would this article convert him — or just help more people to ignore his message and authority? Actually, if there is anybody who has forgotten himself and poured himself out to bring Christ to the world, no matter what the cost, it's John Paul II. I'd call him one of the most Christocentric people on the face of the earth!

But, in any case, he's our leader. He's the center of unity for the Church, and if we want to fulfill the command of the Lord and build up the body of Christ in unity, we need to rally around him and try to encourage all the followers of the Lord to do the same. And what we say of John Paul II, we say of the bishops in union with him and the pastors in union with those bishops. That's God's way for the unity of the Church. Why do we think we know a better one?

Chapter 7

A PAPA FOR THE FAMILY

"The gates of hell shall not prevail!" (Mt 16:18)

I t was the feast of Sts. Peter and Paul, and I was proclaiming the Gospel for the day. It was one I had read and heard and talked about many, many times: "You are Peter and upon this rock I will build my church, and the gates of the netherworld shall not prevail against it" (Mt 16:18). What struck me this day, however, was *the connection between "the gates of hell" not prevailing against the Church and the role of Peter. This promise of Jesus is tied up with His appointment of Peter as the rock. If we have seen "the gates of hell" get a foothold in the Church, could it not well be because too many of us have been ignoring or neglecting or playing down the place of Peter and his successors?*

I don't know why some outside of the Catholic Church and some inside have such a big problem with recognizing the Pope. Basically it comes down to this. Purposeful groups in society normally have a leader. You form a card club or a hunting club or a parish council, and you choose a head. A country, a school, a legislature — they all elect or appoint someone to lead. In marriage and the family, the smallest and most basic unit of society, there is a need for headship.

Now if Jesus wanted His Church to continue in this world of us human beings — and especially if He wanted us to be together — He would have done the most natural thing in the world. He would have appointed one of the apostles as the leader of the rest. And we see that that's exactly what He did.

From the Gospels and the Acts of the Apostles and the Epistles — it is Peter who clearly and unmistakably emerges as the leader of the twelve apostles and of the Christian community. He is referred to by name 182 times in the New Testament. Second runner-up for frequent mention among the apostles is John — with a whopping 34 times! Peter is the one who is always named first in the listings of the twelve (Mt 10:2; Mk 3:16; Lk 6:14; Acts 1:13). He's the one also named first among those whom Jesus took with Him into the garden of Gethsemani and onto the mount of Tabor. Right after the ascension of Jesus, the apostles and disciples gather together in the cenacle at Jerusalem awaiting the promised Holy Spirit. As a body of believers they take their first concerted action to elect someone to replace Judas — and who is it that initiates that action? In Chapter 1 of Acts, we read these words: "During those days Peter stood up in the midst of the brothers . . ." (v. 15). It was Peter who called for that election.

It was Peter too who on the day of Pentecost takes the leadership as the Church begins her preaching mission. "Peter stood up with the Eleven, raised his voice, and proclaimed to them . . ." (Acts 2:14). This is a symbol of what the Church of all time is meant to be and do through the successors of Peter and the apostles — the Pope and the bishops with him: to stand up in the world and proclaim a strong clear message to the ends of the earth and give a witness of unity of faith and love.

The words of Jesus to Peter regarding his special role among the apostles and for the Church are considerable. To go into them thoroughly would take a whole book in itself, the kind scholars (not I!) have written. But some appreciation of them is important for us here. First of all, when He called him to be an apostle, as we find at the beginning of John's gospel, He changed his name from Simon to Peter. "Jesus looked at him and said, 'You are Simon the son of John; you will be called Kephas (which is translated Peter)'" (Jn 1:42). In biblical times a name change signified a special characteristic or new mission of the person so named. We see this in the case of Israel and Abraham. Abraham's name, for example, was Abram. God gave him the name Abraham when He called him to be "the father of a host of nations," which the name signifies (Gn 17:5). The name Peter, or in Aramaic Kephas, is striking. We have no record in antiquity of anyone else being given that name. [1] The name means "rock". Certainly Peter , who got afraid on the waters and began to sink, and Peter, who denied that he ever knew the Lord the night of His arrest, was no rock by nature! But Jesus is giving him a rock-like mission in His Church — to be its central earthly foundation stone and secure guardian of the faith.

One of the scriptural images of the Church is a building. We are a building made up of "living stones" (1 Pet 2:5-6). Jesus is the cornerstone. He is no longer, however, visible to us, and Jesus wanted His Church to be a visible organization. So He, the builder, laid a visible foundation stone that would remain after Him through Peter and his successors. All the apostles are foundation stones of the Church "built upon the foundation of the apostles" (Eph 2:20), but especially Peter as the chief and central stone. "You are Peter, and upon *this rock* I will build my Church" (Mt 16:18).

The "I will build" of Jesus continues to this day. He is still building His Church and we the living stones make up the building as a temple of the Holy Spirit (1 Pet 2:5-6). The living stones are still being added to the structure as new members come into the Church through baptism. To be fully joined to His Church, however, we need to be connected with the central stone—Peter, the rock and his successors—around which the visible structure is being built.

The text is clear enough, but it has been twisted to say other things. Some even picture Jesus saying to Peter, "You are rock," but then pointing to Himself and adding "and upon this rock (Me) I will build my church!" More seriously, however, others claim that it is Peter's profession of faith that is the rock on which Christ builds, and not Peter himself. The argument used to back this up is that in the Greek language employed by the Gospel writers the word for rock is *petra* and the name Jesus gave to Peter is **Petros** which in Greek literally means "little rock." In the Greek translation, therefore, we read: "You are **Petros** and on this **petra** I will build my Church."

A simple answer to this is that Jesus did not speak Greek but Aramaic. In the Aramaic language there is no such distinction. The word is **Kepha**; and Jesus would have said, "You are **Kepha** and upon this **Kepha** I will build my church." When this dialogue is translated into the Greek language, Jesus does not say "You are *Petra*" simply because *petra* is a feminine name. *Petros* is the masculine equivalent. Otherwise, we would have to translate his name in English as Petrilla or Rockette!

In any case, why not simply say that the text refers to Peter with his faith or to the faith embodied in Peter? Certainly it does not refer to Peter the man left completely to himself. We see what he did when left to himself! But it refers to Peter the man aided by the grace of God because Jesus says, about his confession of faith, "For flesh and blood has not revealed this to you, but my heavenly Father" (Mt. 16:17).

Thank God that today more and more Protestant scholars are admitting that Jesus is truly referring to Peter as the rock of His Church. In fact, it's getting to be the majority. [2] An example of this is Herman Ritterbos' recent commentary on this text from his book called Matthew. Ritterbos is a world-renowned, Bible-believing Protestant commentator. He says,"because the feminine ending of this noun made it unsuitable as a man's name, however, Simon was not called *Petra* but *Petros* .... There's no good reason to think that Jesus switched from *Petros* to *Petra* to show that He was not speaking of the man Peter but of his confession as the foundation of the church. The words *'on this rock (Petra)' indeed refer to Peter.* Because of the revelation that he had received and the confession that it motivated in him, *Peter was appointed by Jesus to lay the foundation of the future Church."* [3]

But there is much more that Jesus said to Peter about his role in the Church besides the words "on this rock." Even in that same context (Mt 16:13-19) Jesus goes on to say, "I will give you the keys of the kingdom of heaven. Whatever you bind on earth shall be bound in heaven; whatever you loose on earth shall be loosed in heaven" (v. 19). In those days, cities were built with a wall around them for protection. I visited Jerusalem and could still see the ancient wall and gates of the city. The one who had control of the keys to the city gates was the one in charge. It's still generally true today in regard to keys. The head of the house, the boss of a company, the pastor of a church is the one who controls the keys.

A footnote to this verse in many editions of the Bible, both Catholic and Protestant, refers to an Old Testament parallel in Isaiah 22:22 from which the image of the keys is probably drawn. Eliakim is chosen to replace the former prime minister of the Davidic kingdom. About him God says: "I will place the key of the House of David on his shoulder; when he opens, no one shall shut; when he shuts, no one will open." Jesus is using this kind of image in addressing Peter.

We sometimes jokingly say, "Peter is up there at the gate. I hope he'll let me in!" That's not what Jesus is saying! He's talking about the kingdom on earth. He goes on to say, "Whatever you declare bound *on earth* shall be bound in heaven; whatever you declare loosed on earth shall be loosed in heaven." *He's giving him a spiritual authority in His kingdom on earth.* "Binding and loosing" was an expression commonly used by the rabbis, the spiritual leaders of Israel. "Of the several meanings . . . two are of special importance here: the giving of authoritative teaching and the lifting or imposing of the ban of excommunication." 4 It is this type of spiritual authority that Jesus is conferring on Peter. On another occasion He entrusts the authority to bind and loose to all the disciples (Mt 18:18), but here in a special way to their leader and to him alone He confers the keys.

In Luke's Gospel, we have another passage in which Jesus says to Peter: "Simon, Simon, behold Satan has demanded to sift all of you like wheat" (22:31). Equivalently, Jesus is saying, in anticipation of His passion and death, "Satan is planning to violently shake your faith and that of all the apostles." But then the Master adds, "but I have prayed that your own faith may not fail; and once you have turned back, *you* must strengthen your brothers" (v. 32). In the context and in the original language of this Gospel there is absolutely no doubt that the *you* here is singular, referring to Peter alone.

That's the role of Peter, and that's the role of the Pope. How prophetically do we see that fulfilled in John Paul II! *To strengthen his fellow bishops, to strengthen his fellow priests, to strengthen all of us in faith — that's his role, and to do that above all in his office as teacher, teacher of true doctrine.* This role of Peter is a special role, but it is fulfilled not by *his* strength but *by the strength and protection of the Lord.* Peter was weak. Peter got afraid. Peter started to sink in the water. Peter denied the Lord. But, "I have prayed that your own faith may not fail" (Lk 22:32).

In other words, Jesus is saying, "I'm going to back you up in believing and teaching and shepherding — and that will be the source of your carrying out your mission." In spite of all his bungling and sins, Peter's clear and bold proclamation of faith in the messiahship and divinity of Jesus, "You are the Messiah, the Son of the living God" (Mt 16:16) — is an expression of this special grace and role

69

given to the chief teacher and shepherd of the Church. "For flesh and blood has not revealed this to you, but my heavenly Father" (Mt 16:17).

In John's Gospel, the last of the four, in his final chapter, we have a beautiful passage where after the resurrection Jesus appears to the apostles and invites them to a breakfast of bread and fish which He had prepared on the shore of the lake. "When they had eaten their meal," Jesus asks Peter three times, "Do you love me?" After each response Jesus says, "Feed my lambs"; "Tend my sheep"; and, finally, "Feed my sheep" (21:15-17). Jesus the "chief Shepherd" (1 Pt 5:4) is about to leave the earth in visible form. Before doing so, He singles out Peter in the presence of all the other apostles to take care of His flock in His name.

All the apostles and their successors are to be shepherds and pastors of the flock of Jesus. Paul uses that image when he addresses the presbyters (priests, elders) in Ephesus: "Keep watch over yourselves and over the whole flock of which the Holy Spirit has appointed you overseers, in which you tend the church of God that he acquired with his own blood" (Acts 20:28). Peter himself writes: "So I exhort the presbyters among you, as a fellow presbyter and witness to the sufferings of Christ and one who has a share in the glory to be revealed. Tend the flock of God in your midst, (overseeing) not by constraint but willingly . . . Do not lord it over those assigned to you, but be examples to the flock. And when the chief Shepherd is revealed, you will receive the unfading crown of glory" (1 Pt 5:1-4).

Jesus remains the great invisible Shepherd, but the flock in this world till the end of time needs many visible shepherds and pastors. One, however, has to take over the

*role of chief, or leader, or central shepherd; and that one,
designated by Jesus and recognized unquestionably by
the early Church, was Peter.*

Many Protestant scholars, like the great Lutheran biblical scholar Oscar Cullmann, in his work called <u>Peter,</u> 5 now
admit without a doubt that he was appointed leader and
recognized as such in the beginning of the Church. They do
not, however, take the next step and see the role of Peter
being passed on to successors. But why not? *Is the Church
in any less need of unity, of strengthening the brethren, of
clear teaching, than in the days of Peter? Actually, it's just
the opposite. We're in an even greater need.* Jesus intended His Church to remain until the end of time. When He
sends the apostles out to bring the Gospel to all the nations
and to baptize, He tells them, "I am with you always, until
the end of the age" (Mt 28-20). If the role of Peter were not
to continue, then why should the role of any of the apostles
or of the Church in general continue — preaching, baptizing, keeping the Supper of the Lord? In the appointment of
Peter, He's leaving a clear plan for the governing and
unifying of His flock, His family, until He comes again.

The Church is a family, the "household of God" (1 Tim
3:15). As every family, it needs a papa, and that's exactly
what the word Pope means. Each parish has its own
pastor who is called father, and the chief pastor is the
father of them all.

The first time I ever saw a Pope in person was as a
young priest when I took part in a public audience with
Pope Pius XII. As we waited excitedly in a large hall for the
Pope to arrive, there was with us in the crowd a group of
Italian seminarians who were singing their hearts out —
happy, enthusiastic and jubilant. The whole atmosphere

was that of a family awaiting its papa. I had heard that it was the custom (in those days, anyway) for people to shout "Viva il papa!" when the Pope came in. As an uptight but "cool" American, I couldn't picture myself doing that. But when the doors opened and the Pope appeared, carried on the "sedia gestatoria," I was so swept away by the enthusiasm and jubilation around me that I was shouting with everyone else! In fact, I pushed my way through the crowd (maybe butting some Italian mammas in the process!) and according to my young brother who was with me, I almost pulled the Pope out of his chair!

It was also this kind of spirit that filled St. Louis Cathedral in New Orleans many years later when John Paul II walked down the aisle, and priests and nuns and other special guests clapped and cheered and stood on pews to see and reach out to him. What I loved so much about it was how unsophisticated it all was—like children at a big surprise birthday party for their papa! How much we need to recapture that childlike family spirit once again throughout the Church in our relationship with one another and with the Pope.

Some years ago I had the opportunity to go to Kenya in Africa. I spent a couple of weeks there, visiting the family members of an African friend in various towns and villages. One thing among others that struck me was this. At that time, Kenyata was president. Everywhere, in homes, in village stores and in institutions, his picture was visible. There was a motto in the country: "Harambee." It's Swahili for "Let's all pull together." It wasn't just that many thought Kenyata personally was great, but the people of Kenya recognized that he was their leader, their center of unity, and that they would never be able to get together unless they rallied around him.

How foolish we Catholics are when we do the opposite in the Church today. Nobody ever said that the Pope was perfect. Everyday at Mass he himself says, "Oh Lord I am not worthy." No Catholic is expected to believe that in all of his policies and day-to-day decisions and statements, he is infallible; but in the providence of God, he is the chief bishop, pastor and teacher in the Church. *A test of whether I'm on the right track in my teaching or practice of faith or morals is: Is it in accord with his teaching and directives?*

It's in the very early days of Christianity, before the first century ends, that we find Clement, Bishop of Rome and successor of St. Peter, writing to Christians in Corinth, Greece, in order to urge them to be obedient to their legitimately ordained bishop and priests and to heal a schism. 6 Clement's intervention had its effect, and the schism was healed. Obviously Clement's influence extended beyond his own immediate city and diocese. A hundred years later Irenaeus, Bishop of Lyons, in his great work entitled, Against Heresies, mentions this letter and writes about "the successions of the bishops of the greatest and most ancient Church known to all, founded and organized at Rome by the two most glorious Apostles, Peter and Paul, that Church which has the tradition and the faith which comes down to us after having been announced to men by the Apostles. *For with this Church, because of its superior origin, all Churches must agree*, that is, all the faithful in the whole world; and it is in her that the faithful everywhere have maintained the Apostolic tradition." 7 These are just two of the many, many evidences of a recognition in early times, as well as of a development in understanding, of the role of the Pope as successor of Peter and visible head of the Church.

How important it is for us to "get it together" today and get behind the man who, above all others, has the role of proclaiming the good news to the ends of the earth, preserving the faith in its integrity and creating harmony and unity in the body of Christ. How much the world needs his voice and his message and to see it backed up by the members of the body of that Church of which he is the visible head! As someone put it: *What would it look like if someday we Catholics would truly rally around the successor of Peter and together with him take a united stand even on any one issue affecting life and the world today? What a witness that would be! What a power for good would be unleashed in our world! Is that not God's vision for His Church?*

Chapter 8

THE HOLY SPIRIT
IN THE CHURCH

Renewing the Church always

"The holy Spirit will come upon you, and the power of the most high will overshadow you . . . for nothing will be impossible for God." We find that promise made to Mary in the first chapter of the Gospel of Luke, verses 35-37. The promise is for the whole Church. It's for you and for me. "The holy Spirit will come upon you . . . nothing will be impossible for God." All the power of the Church comes from Jesus' greatest gift to us — the gift of the Holy Spirit. It was the gift Jesus promised He would send to His Church when He left the earth. The Holy Spirit is truly "the soul of the Church", and all the gifts of the Spirit that the Church needs to carry on her mission are given as we continue to surrender ourselves to the Spirit in the attitude of Mary, "I am the handmaid of the Lord. May it be done to me according to your word" (v. 38).

There is a prayer that I used to pray as a child, a prayer my parents prayed and that I learned from the parochial school and church that I attended, a prayer that has been on the lips of Catholic people for generations: "Come Holy Spirit, fill the hearts of Your faithful and enkindle in us the fire of Your love. Send forth Your Spirit and we shall be (re)created and You shall renew the face of the earth." Something is different, however, when I say that prayer now, different from when I used to pray it as a child and even as a younger priest. *Now I expect much more! I truly expect the Holy Spirit to enkindle a fire in my heart and to light a fire on this earth!* One reason that I expect that is because I have seen, in a new way, the work of the Spirit in my own life and in the lives of countless people whom I've met and whom I've heard about on the face of the earth today.

Parish priests look forward to the day when they will be appointed pastors, and I looked forward to that day. When I was younger and worked as an assistant with other pastors, I sometimes thought, "Hey, I could do it better than this guy!" (Now I can identify with the newly appointed pastor who said: "You know, it's funny but shortly after I got to be a pastor, my whole attitude toward pastors changed!") But in those days I thought about things that I'd like to do in a parish when I became pastor. I had plans and dreams of what I wanted to accomplish. Finally the day came when the Archbishop called me in and appointed me to my first pastorate, and I was a happy man. It was like a whole new world opening up to me.

What I noticed, however, as the months and years went by was that many of those plans and dreams were not being worked out. It was in the 60s when I was appointed pastor, and, among other problems, there were tense and unjust race relations. I've always believed (what my Catholic parents and Church taught me): that preaching and practicing social and interracial justice is part and parcel of the Christian life and message. I've also believed that if we can't learn to live and work together as brothers and sisters in our Church organizations and parish life, how can we ever hope to realize this in the world around us?

It seemed, however, the more I tried to bring this about at first in the parish and then in the community at large, the more effort I made, the worse things got. Even in our own parish staff we were getting bogged down (for other than racial reasons), and it looked like I just couldn't "make it fly". Also around that time I got sick. I was hit with a bad case of the flu that drained me physically. Even after I got over it, I felt as if I couldn't get my strength back, that I had lost my drive. With all of this put together, I began to feel like a washout, a failure. I was questioning myself, my ability, my manhood.

For years I've belonged to a support group of priests, the "Jesus Caritas" fraternity. At one of our gatherings, I was sharing the way that I felt. There was a priest there that day who was new to the group. He had become involved in the Catholic Charismatic Renewal. After our meeting he offered to pray with me an inner-healing prayer, a healing of memories. He asked me if the way that I felt right at that time was bringing back feelings, memories from the past. I said, "Yes," and mentioned some of the memories and feelings that were being stirred up inside of me. He prayed a prayer, placing his hands on my head, asking Jesus to go back into those memories and emotions and bring His healing love to bear upon each of them. Then he prayed that the Holy Spirit would strengthen me and lift me up. When he finished his prayer, he asked, "How do you feel?"

"To tell you the truth," I said, "I felt funny about you being that close to me (I wasn't used to letting people get that close!) and I felt pretty eerie about someone praying over me the way you did! (wary of faith healers and traiteurs). But as you ended your prayer, I felt something like a gentle healing Spirit moving inside of me and I'd just like to be alone for a while and pray."

That was a new experience in my life — the beginning of a new awareness of the closeness and power of God. Sometime after that I went on vacation and in connection with that vacation I read some books about the Holy Spirit. I had studied about the Spirit. I thought I knew about the Holy Spirit. But what was different in these books was the stories of real live people of today and what happened to them when they surrendered their lives to Jesus as Lord and opened themselves to the power of the Holy Spirit.

One was the little book The Cross and the Switchblade, [1] about the young clergyman who felt inspired to go into New York city and work with gangs of teenagers hung up on dope, sex, or violence. With fear and trembling, but trusting in the power of God, he reached out to these young people. Lives began to change; something new began to happen and kids addicted even to hard drugs were set free as he invited them to open their lives to Jesus and to His Spirit. I wasn't used to freely expressing my emotions in those days. (I had grown up in a "boys/men don't cry" environment.) As I read this little book, however, tears welled up in my eyes. I could identify with that minister. I had experienced my own weakness and helplessness and had come to know in a new way how much I needed the power of God.

When I got back home from that vacation, but before I went back to the parish, I met with a priest friend who had started a small charismatic prayer group; and he brought me over to meet the leader of that group. I remember that day as we sat in the parlor of this lady's home, and they shared with me what was happening in that small prayer group as they came together week after week and opened their lives to the Spirit. Before I left the house, I was inspired to do something that I hadn't planned on doing. I asked them to pray over me.

I told them something like this, "You know, the day I was baptized, the day that I was confirmed, the day that I was ordained, I believe that I received special outpourings of the Holy Spirit; but in those days I didn't know how much I needed the Holy Spirit. Maybe, in the back of my mind (when I was old enough to think), I thought that I could do it by my power with a little help from God! But now I know what I didn't know then, that I can't do it; but I believe that God can do it and that if I could just let go and let God take over, if I could get out of the way, as it were, and let God do all that He wants to do, then it will happen."

I knelt down and they gathered around me, this mother of a family, this priest friend, and a young student who came in at that time who belonged to the prayer group. They put their hands on me, and they prayed for a new outpouring of the Holy Spirit in my life. I remember one of them said, "You're asking to die!" (i.e., to yourself so that God can take over).

Do you know what happened? ... Nothing! I went away from that house as dry as dry bones. But the next morning when I woke up, I was singing! That was a miracle in itself.

I'm not a "morning" person. I can stay up late at night but hate to get up early in the morning, and especially in those days I didn't feel like singing when I got up in the morning! But, as I remember it, that morning I even began singing in my dream before I opened my eyes! And there was inside of me, even physically, the sensation of a little fire burning — like a pilot light that had been lit in the middle of my heart, something I recalled experiencing shortly after they prayed over me.

When I got back to the parish a few days after that, I realized that there was something different in my life. There was a new joy and enthusiasm in my work as a priest. There was a new realization that God was not a million miles away, but that He was right here with me and inside me. There was a new power to love the people that I had been called to serve, and there was a new acceptance and love of myself as God had made me. There was a new thanksgiving that was welling up in my heart, thanking God for everything — eventually, even the difficult things. As I would pick up the Bible, things that I had read many times seemed to take on a new depth of meaning.

I noticed too that there was a new power in my life and that it wasn't any power that I had of myself. I wasn't relying as much on my own resources as on His, and He was honoring that. I had moved aside, at least a little bit, and God was doing what He had always wanted to do and I wasn't blocking Him (as much!).

Ever since then, there has been a burning desire in my heart to share with all my brothers and sisters, and especially my brothers and sisters in the Catholic Church, the good news about the Holy Spirit. In a sense, it's nothing really new. I've always believed and we Catholics have always believed in the Holy Spirit. As a child, I learned to make the Sign of the Cross: "In the name of the Father, and of the Son and of the Holy Spirit." As a young boy I learned the prayer song: "Come Holy Ghost". At ordination to the priesthood, I had a card printed for family and friends that had on it a prayer to the Holy Spirit by Cardinal Mercier. Through the years of my priesthood I have said that prayer, sometimes several times a day — a prayer of surrender to the Holy Spirit asking His guidance, praying to be submissive to Him in everything. *But what's new now is that when I pray that prayer or any prayer to the Holy Spirit, I am more aware of what the Holy Spirit can do, of the renewal that He can give.*

My experience is that of only one among millions of Catholics and non-Catholics, in our day, who have experienced anew the power, the renewal of the Holy Spirit — in and outside of the Charismatic Movement. Many of them talk about it as "baptism in the Spirit", as a new immersion in the Spirit. We can only be baptized with water once, but the effect of that baptism can be realized in our lives more and more as life goes along, as we continue to surrender to the power of God. As Catholics we can only be confirmed or ordained to the priesthood once, but the effect of that confirmation or ordination, the grace of those sacraments can be continually stirred up within us. As St. Paul says, "I remind you to stir into flame the gift of God that you have through the imposition of my hands" (2 Tm 1:6), urging Timothy to let be renewed within him the power of the Spirit given in ordination.

I believe in all the sanctifying gifts of the Holy Spirit, seven of which are proclaimed in Isaiah, the prophet: Wisdom, Understanding, Counsel, Fortitude, Knowledge, Piety, and Fear of the Lord (11:2-3). I believe in all the charismatic and service gifts, some of which we hear about in Paul's first Letter to the Corinthians: "There are different kinds of spiritual gifts but the same Spirit; there are different forms of service but the same Lord; there are different workings but the same God who produces all of them in everyone. To each individual the manifestation of the Spirit is given for some benefit. To one is given through the Spirit the expression of wisdom; to another the expression of knowledge according to the same Spirit; to another faith by the same Spirit; to another gifts of healing by the one Spirit; to another mighty deeds; to another prophecy; to another discernment of spirits; to another varieties of tongues; to another interpretation of tongues. But one and the same Spirit produces all of these, distributing them individually to each person as he wishes" (12:4-11).

I believe in the wonderful character traits produced by the Spirit as described in Paul's Letter to the Galatians, "The fruit of the Spirit is love, joy, peace, patience, kindness, generosity, faithfulness, gentleness, self-control" (5:22-23).

Wow! The Holy Spirit can really do something! And I have seen that all of this is for real. I realize now that that was the secret of what happened in Mary, the Mother of Jesus, and *the secret of what happened to all the saints. They were men and women and young people like us but they were truly open to, surrendered to, and moved by — the Spirit. It wasn't their power, but the power of God working in them. In their lives the gifts of the Spirit and the fruits of the Spirit were very much alive and evident.*

It is true that for many centuries in the history of the Church some of the charismatic gifts were de-emphasized and even looked upon with suspicion. But a closer study indicates that they were never completely absent from the life of the Church and, thank God, today are coming to the fore more than ever. This is true especially through the Catholic Charismatic Renewal. Some Catholics, however, wonder about the authenticity of this renewal: *Is it truly Catholic?*

Certainly, as in every movement that has ever existed in the Church, there are those who go to extremes and misrepresent its true purpose and meaning. The bishops of our country, however, and the Popes of our Church, have endorsed the Catholic Charismatic Renewal. Three times the bishops of the United States created a commission to study and then to work with this renewal, and three times they have encouraged it while giving guidelines and cautions for its activities and development. Pope Paul VI met with 10,000 participants of the International Conference of the Catholic Charismatic Renewal from different parts of the world in 1975 around the main altar of St. Peter's Basilica in Rome. He addressed them encouragingly and called the renewal a hope for the Church or a "chance for the Church." "How could this 'spiritual renewal' not be a chance for the Church and the world?" he asked. [2]

The renewal is an opportunity for the Church, "a chance", a time of grace and visitation; but it's up to us not to miss it! I think of Jesus' words as He wept over Jerusalem, "you did not recognize the time of your visitation" (Lk 19:44). Our present Pope, John Paul II, has called the Catholic Charismatic Movement "a particular gift of the Holy Spirit to the Church" [3] and has said he looks to movements like this for the renewal of the Church. He has several times met with leaders of this renewal and blessed and encouraged them in what they were doing.

Regarding priests, he has said, "The priest, for his part, cannot exercise his service on behalf of the (Charismatic) renewal unless and until he adopts a welcoming attitude toward it, based on the desire he shares with every Christian by baptism to grow in the gifts of the Holy Spirit." [4] In all of their statements the bishops of our country have also been urging priests to give pastoral guidance to this renewal. They echo the words just quoted and they also say, *"Insofar as the renewal makes its own what is central to the enduring reality of the Gospel, it cannot be dismissed as peripheral to the life of the Church. Clearly the charismatic renewal is in and for the Church, not alongside the Church."* [5]

You don't need to belong to a movement, however, in order to be open to the Spirit. *The movement might not be for everyone but what the movement is pointing to, renewal in the Spirit, baptism in the Spirit — is for everyone.* As shown by a recent study, baptism in the Holy Spirit, often manifested by various charisms, was regularly connected with the reception of converts into the Church for the first four centuries and to some extent even up to the ninth century. It was part of "normal" Christianity. [6]

The world and the Church of our day need more than anything a new outpouring of the Holy Spirit. "We must be convinced that a deepened awareness of the person and work of the Holy Spirit responds to the needs of our times", says John Paul II, "for the Spirit 'is at the center of the Christian Faith and is the source and dynamic power of the Church's renewal.' Indeed, the Holy Spirit is 'the principal agent of the Church's mission,' sustaining and guiding her efforts to bring the graces of Pentecost to all people."7 The prayer of Pope John XXIII at the beginning of Vatican II is a prayer for every age and every day and every person: "Renew your wonders in this, our day, as by a new Pentecost."

All the gifts of the Spirit inflamed by the supreme gift, the fire of love (1 Cor 13-14: 1) *are needed by the whole Church for its upbuilding and mission.* Everyone of us needs to be wide open to whatever gifts God wants to give. The world of today, with great urgency, needs to see the power of God, the witness of people moved by God, and the working of God in the lives of those around them!

When I was a student preparing for the priesthood, I would sometimes ask in class, "Why is it so many of the things we read about in the life of Jesus and of the early Church like healings, tongues, miracles, why is it we don't see more of that today?" The traditional answer was (and I understand it was the answer in many Protestant seminaries as well)"Well, the Church was just getting started and those things were needed back at that time; but we don't need them today". I wasn't satisfied with that answer when I heard it then and I certainly don't accept it now. If there were ever a day and time when we needed those gifts and signs, it's today — when faith is growing cold and such great darkness is engulfing so many parts of the earth and even the Church. I believe that God is today working "signs and wonders" (Acts 4:30). He's offering and pouring out His gifts on the Church and the world and we need to be crying with our whole heart: "Come Holy Spirit, fill the hearts of Your people and enkindle in them, enkindle in us, the fire of Your love!"

Catholics don't need to leave the Catholic Church in order to find the Holy Spirit. He is the soul of the Church. He is right in the bosom of the Church. *"There can be no conflict between fidelity to the Spirit and fidelity to the Church and her magisterium"*, says Pope John Paul II. [8] All we need to do is to send up day after day, with expectant faith the earnest plea, "Come Holy Spirit!" and say with Mary, "I am the handmaid of the Lord. May it be done to me according to your word" (Lk 1:38) — surrendering ourselves anew every day to the Spirit of the living God.

One thing the Holy Spirit has done in my own life is to give me an ever deepening appreciation of the mystery of the Church. Ages ago St. Augustine said "A man possesses the Holy Spirit to the measure of his love for Christ's Church". [9] The Spirit has lighted up for me all the treasures of my Catholic faith: the Mass, the power of the Holy Eucharist and of each of the sacraments, a new appreciation of the priesthood, of celibacy and of marriage and family life as well, devotion to the saints and especially to Our Blessed Lady, the call to daily conversion and purification and the meaning of purgatory, the need for the guidance of the Church and the importance of the Church's defense of human life, human sexuality, and human dignity - the dignity of every person on the face of the earth. *I wonder about those who "get the spirit" and then get out of the Church (overtly or covertly). I wonder what spirit they got! If it's genuinely the Holy Spirit, once we surrender to Him, surrender to God, it's important that we surrender to and follow the guidance of the same Spirit in the Church.*

We do need the Church to teach us rightly about the ways of the Spirit. You and I might sincerely surrender to the Holy Spirit, and yet as time goes along be greatly deceived without the Church. The Spirit wants to guide us personally but also through the legitimate authority of the Church. *It is possible (and we see it all over the place) for anyone of us to be led astray if we rely simply on our own personal understanding of what the Spirit wants to say.*

How many times have you and I run across people who have done such foolish and destructive things saying, "God told me to do it!" How much we need to check our personal guidance against the guidance that God gives to His Church around the world. How much we need, as St. Paul tells us, to "not quench the Spirit ... (but) Test everything!" (1 Thes 5:19-21). One of the best tests is to ask ourselves: "Is this in accord with what the Spirit is saying to the Church and to those who have been commissioned to guide us in the name of Jesus Christ as the legitimately appointed shepherds of His Church in union with the chief shepherd, the successor of Peter?" It is their job, as Paul reminds the shepherds of his day to "keep watch over yourselves and over the whole flock of which the Holy Spirit has appointed you overseers . . . " (Acts 20:28).

Clearly Jesus warns against just looking for special manifestations of God's power without doing the will of God. In Matthew's Gospel we read these words: "Every tree that does not bear good fruit will be cut down and thrown into the fire. So by their fruits you will know them. Not everyone who says to me, 'Lord, Lord,' will enter the kingdom of heaven, but only the one who does the will of my Father in heaven. Many will say to me on that day, 'Lord, Lord did we not prophesy in your name? Did we not drive out demons in your name? Did we not do mighty deeds in your name?' Then I will declare to them solemnly, 'I never knew you. Depart from me, you evildoers'" (7:19-23).

How applicable to those of us who believe so much in all these charismatic gifts of the Spirit: the gift of prophesy, the gift of casting out demons, the gift of miracles in the name of the Lord and other gifts as well. Jesus says that you can do all those things and yet not inherit the kingdom of God. You could do all those things and still merit the condemnation: "I never knew you. Depart from me you evildoers" because the test is "Not everyone who says to me, Lord, Lord, will enter the kingdom of heaven but only the one who does the will of my Father in heaven".

To do the will of God we need to know God's will very clearly. We need to know what He wants us to believe and what He wants us to do. And, so we won't be deceived, He gave us the Church to guide us in His name — a Church guided by the Spirit with authority to teach clearly in matters that have to do with our faith and moral lives.

In the words of Pope John XXIII, let's continually acknowledge and pray: *"O Holy Spirit, sent by the Father in the name of Jesus, you are present in the Church, guiding it infallibly. We pray you to pour forth the fullness of your gifts . . . Renew your wonders in this, our day, as by a new Pentecost. Grant that your Church, persevering in prayer with Mary, the Mother of Jesus, united in heart and mind, and led by Saint Peter, may extend the Divine Savior's reign of truth and justice, love, and peace."*[10]

Chapter 9

FIVE OTHER MARKS
OF THE CHURCH

Traditional and Innovative

As far back as the Council of Constantinople, in the year 381 of the Christian era, four characteristic marks of the Church were spelled out in the creed promulgated by this Council. Every Sunday in the words of that creed, we stand up and profess our faith in the "one, holy, catholic, and apostolic Church."

This side of heaven, the pilgrim Church, made up of us sinful human beings, falls short of realizing the first three of these marks in a perfect way. They are more of a goal towards which we are always to strive rather than something already achieved. Yet even with all their imperfections these marks are still present enough in the Catholic Church to show that it is the one to which God is calling His people. They are tremendous gifts of God for which we should thank Him with all our heart and pray and work that they might grow and increase in our midst.

The Catholic Church is **ONE** worldwide Church with *one central visible head*, the Pope; with the bishops united with that head; with *one common faith; one common worship.* Wherever you go in the world and in all different languages and cultures of the earth, there is *one central act of worship,* the Mass. There are *the same seven sacraments,* those effective signs Jesus gave us. There is also *clear official teaching* on matters of faith and morals — regardless of the disagreements of theologians and teachers and rank and file members.

Jesus prayed that as the Father and He are one, "that they may all be one . . . that the world may believe that you sent me" (Jn 17:21). Now God knows that we often divide from one another in the Church on important issues and even on petty things. In parish life and organizations, at times, we create division and don't give that perfect sign of unity. So we're always yearning for a more perfect unity. But basically it does exist and the structure is there for it to grow. We thank God for that and see it as a sign that this is the Church of the Lord.

HOLINESS. The Church's holiness is primarily because of her Head and Soul (the Holy Spirit), and holiness is her very purpose. Christ, "as head [of] . . . the church, which is his body" (Eph 1:22-23), "loved the church and handed himself over for her *to sanctify her*, cleansing her by the bath of water with the word, that he might present to himself the church in splendor, without spot or wrinkle or any such thing, *that she might be holy* and without blemish" (Eph 5:25-27). *Everything in the life of the Church is meant ultimately to lead to the salvation and sanctification of its members and of the world* — to an ever-deepening union with Jesus Christ and openness to His Spirit.

The Church is also holy in its *models*, its *means*, and its *members*. The Catholic Church holds up for us continually, at the center of everything, the great *model* Jesus Christ, "The way, the truth and the life" (Jn 14:6), and also Mary and the saints who followed Him and reflect His holiness, as the moon reflects the light of the sun. The Church also offers us the *means* of genuine holiness in her liturgy and devotional life, her activities and associations — but especially in the Holy Eucharist and all the sacraments. She also gives evidence of the good fruit of holiness in lives of her *members*. It's true, we may often look around and say, "But I see so many faults in the members and leaders of the Church!" Side by side with them, however, are the countless other members and leaders whose lives are truly holy. Would that more and more attention be given to these usually unsung, day-by-day, beautiful people of God!

Now, and down through the history of the Church, in every age, there have also been the people of extraordinary and heroic virtue. They are the saints (canonized and uncanonized) who have lived the Christian, Catholic life, been filled with the Spirit of the Lord, and are signs to us of what happens when you really follow Jesus in His Church as they did. You're fired up with the love of the Lord and of neighbor. They witness that she is the Lord's Church and that the means of holiness are there if we choose to use them.

CATHOLIC. We find in the Bible that "it was in Antioch that the disciples were first called Christians" (Acts 11:26). It was Ignatius, bishop of that same city, in a letter to Christians at Smyrna (Turkey), about the year 110 A.D., who first called the Christian Church by the name

Catholic. "Wherever the bishop appears, let the people be there; just as wherever Jesus Christ is, there is the Catholic Church." [1] The word implies that the Church is not just confined to one race or culture or language or part of the world. She's spread out over the earth. She's universal; that's what the word "Catholic" means. She's the Church adaptable to every culture, language and race without alteration or compromise of her teachings — and that is a sign that she's God's Church, Christ's Church.

And then, finally, APOSTOLIC. There is no other beginning for the Church to which we belong than with Jesus and the apostles and Peter. No reputable encyclopedia or history book would ever make any other claim. Our roots are right there in the Gospels and Epistles and Acts of the Apostles. The Catholic Church continues from there to our day in an unbroken line, and that too is a sign that she is true.

Over the years, however, *I've come to recognize five other outstanding marks of the true Church* and I want to say something about them as well. This was brought home to me especially during a sabbatical in 1982. I'm a parish priest, and up until then my work as a priest was primarily parish work. At that time I was granted permission to do a full-time "ministry of the word" (Acts 6:4) under the title of "preaching and spiritual renewal." In preparation for this and as a time of renewal for myself, I was granted a six-month sabbatical. I went off with a carload of books and a whole program of study including some formal university classes and lectures. What I learned in those six months, however, had little or nothing to do with the books or classes or lectures! They were things that God put into my head and heart in prayer and through experiences that happened to me during that time. He sent me back home with the conviction that I had to share these realities with my brothers and sisters. Writing this book is one way of doing that.

The realities impressed upon me during those months had to do with Our Lady, the Eucharist, the Pope and the Church, the Cross and the importance of the Church's teaching on respect for life and the act of love that leads to life. In a modern and ecumenical age these truths are the very ones that Catholics often downplay or sweep under the rug so that we won't appear too different or even odd to those who are not Catholic. I've come to see them, however, as priceless gifts of God — treasures of faith — to be shared out of love with all who will accept them and with a world that needs and even unconsciously longs for them so badly. Rightly understood they are great means of spiritual revitalization — and even bridges for unity among all Christians. I've also come to see them as five additional marks or signs (especially when taken together) of the truth of the Catholic Church. I'll briefly touch on each of them, as listed here, in the final chapters of this book.

MARY — The Bible says,
    "They found the child *with Mary* his Mother"
    (Mt 2:11)(unrevised edition)
EUCHARIST — Jesus says,
    "This *is* my body...this *is* my blood (Mt 26:26-28/
    Mk14:22-24/Lk 22:19-20).
THE POPE — Christian tradition says,
    "Where Peter is — *there* is the Church"

THE CROSS — St. Paul says,

"We proclaim Christ *crucified*" (1 Cor 1:23)

LIFE AND THE ACT OF LOVE THAT LEADS TO LIFE — Mother Teresa says,

> *"The great destroyer of peace today is the crime against the innocent unborn child..."*. A report at the Congress of the World Federation of Doctors Who Respect Human Life adds: "As we know today, *contraception and abortion are closely linked*, not only ... in respect to their mechanisms, but above all ideologically and psychologically".[2]

Chapter 10

WHY MARY?
ISN'T JESUS ENOUGH?

"They found the child *with Mary* his mother." (Mt 2:11)

Would not the true Church be one that is true to the commandment of the Lord: "Honor your father and your mother" — the only one of the ten commandments that has a specific earthly blessing attached to it? Wouldn't Jesus do that for His own mother and want us to do the same? Would it not be a Church that fulfills the ancient prophecy of Mary "behold, from now on all ages will call me blessed" (Lk 1:48)? Wouldn't it be a Church that repeats the biblical praises of Mary expressed by God's angel and by Elizabeth "inspired by the Holy Spirit": "Hail, favored one (full of grace)! The Lord is with you . . . Blessed are you among women and blessed is the fruit of your womb" (Lk. 1:28, 42)? Would it not also be a Church that perceives the scriptural and providential role of Mary as the first to be touched by Jesus Christ both physically and spiritually — the model of all who would ever be called to open their lives to Him and become participants in His mission and His Church?

It was during that sabbatical of 1982 that I made a trip with the primarily black gospel choir from my last pastorate, which had been invited to sing at a number of different places in France. Towards the end of the journey we hoped to travel down to the town of Lourdes not to give a concert but as pilgrims. On the flight over, someone had shared with me a <u>Reader's Digest</u> article about this shrine. It stated that of all the places of religious pilgrimages on this earth, including Rome, Jerusalem and Mecca — there is none that draws more people than that spot in the Pyrenees where Our Blessed Lady appeared to Bernadette, a 14-year-old peasant girl. We were in Lourdes only one afternoon and evening and left early the next morning. I remember the words that were ringing in my heart as the bus pulled off from that little town: *"Bob, if you're interested in spiritual renewal, don't neglect My mother, for, I'm using her to bring my people back to Me and to be renewed in Me."*

The new surge of Marian devotion since that time and the reports of apparitions — in Medjugorje, the Ukraine, Africa, Japan, and other parts of the world — seem to confirm these words. I've witnessed, over the years that truly God is using Mary in a remarkable, powerful way as an instrument of conversion, evangelization and spiritual renewal. Through her, God's people are being called back to Jesus and His Church; Christians are being called to a greater unity; Christians and non-Christians are called to know and love one another and the world is being called (in spite of many set-backs) to a new unity and peace. To me when a Church recognizes the place of Our Lady in Christian life and the life of the world today — it is at least one of the signs that it is truly the Church of Our Lord. It is still his plan, as in the beginning, that we find "the child *with Mary* his mother" (Mt 2:11).

For years of my own life, even most of my life as a student for the priesthood, I had no personal devotion to Mary. I went through the motions but did not understand the meaning of it all and why it was important. It seemed to me that Jesus was enough. But then one night just about a year before ordination I prayed a prayer to Our Lady, saying something like this, "Mary, you know I don't have devotion to you. I don't even understand why I should pray to you. It seems Jesus is enough. But I know I'm missing something and I ask you to pray for me that I might understand." (Try that sometime, if you're in the same fix and mean it from your heart.) That prayer in the night was a turning point for me. Beginning a few months after that prayer things began to happen in my life and doors of understanding began to open, to this day, that have progressively led me to Our Lady — but always through her more closely to Jesus and His Church. Much of this I've been able to express in a published, personal testimony about Mary called <u>Mary at My side</u>. 1

The first realization that came to me was that God did not have to choose Mary — any more than He had to choose anyone of us or anyone at all to fulfill His plan. He didn't even *have to* send His Son. But in the plan of salvation in which God would take flesh and become one of us, Mary was involved as His Mother. *God chose to use her to be the one through whom the Savior would come into this world. And He still uses her as one through whom the world comes to the Savior. She was associated with Him in His mission on earth and she is still associated with Him in His continuing mission in heaven.*

As a young newly-ordained priest I witnessed this most vividly when I had my first opportunity to go to Lourdes. We arrived late in the afternoon, checked into a little hotel and then rushed over to the grotto for the evening candle-light procession. My eyes popped open with wonder as I watched and took part in this nightly gathering assembled from all over the world carrying the lighted candles (a symbol of Jesus the light of the world), praying the rosary and singing the "Aves" to Mary.

After the procession wended its way through the grounds, it stopped in front of the huge Lourdes basilica and the whole throng with one voice and in the common language of Latin together proclaimed the creed of Christian and Catholic faith. Then the doors of the basilica opened (the custom in those days) and that whole mass of humanity surged into the basilica for Benediction of the Blessed Sacrament. To me it was like a dramatic portrayal of the role of Our Lady in the life of the Church and the world today. *She gathers her children together from all corners of the earth and brings them to Jesus* — to renew their allegiance to Him and His Church and fall down in adoration before Him. The experience of the Magi, representing the nations of the earth, was being repeated again as people found "the child with Mary his mother . . . and did him homage" (Mt 2:11). Like the star of Bethlehem, she leads us to Jesus and His Church.

The subsequent visits to Lourdes, Fatima, Guadalupe, and other places of apparitions of Our Lady have confirmed the impression that struck me that night as a young priest. The center of devotion is not Our Lady but Our Lord. At Lourdes, for example, throughout the day many people spend periods of prayer in the quiet and reverence of the adoration chapel where the Blessed Sacrament of the Body and Blood of the Lord is publicly venerated, take part in the Masses offered several times daily, listen to the proclamation of God's Holy Word and visit in great numbers the reconciliation chapel where confessions are heard in many different languages, being reconciled with God, His Church, and one another. Each afternoon there is the gathering of the sick, many of whom are rolled out in wheelchairs and stretchers to receive the blessing of Our Lord in the Blessed Sacrament — a beautiful witness of both love of God and neighbor since each invalid is assisted by a volunteer. Most of the healings that take place at Lourdes — those that pass the grueling examination of the famed "medical bureau" — most of these are the healings that occur during this eucharistic blessing.

Marian devotion, rightly understood and practiced, is Christ-centered. Her great desire is, as she says in the Gospel, that you and I "Do whatever he tells you" (Jn 2:5). *A realization that came to me over the years was that the passages in the Bible about Mary are there not just to tell us about Mary but also about ourselves. The way she responded to Jesus and the plan of salvation is given to us as a model for all time.* From the first "May it be done to me" (Lk 1:38) to her standing below the cross (Jn 19:25-27) and her prayer with the Church in the cenacle awaiting the Holy Spirit (Acts 1:14) — she is presented as "the first Christian," and model and mother of all who would after her follow Jesus Christ.

She was the closest to Him in body and spirit and, as queen of "the communion of saints," she intercedes with her Son for all His brothers and sisters, who are spiritually her children as well. A great grace for me during the sabbatical was that of entrusting myself, my priesthood and ministry, and my commitment to celibacy — to her special care and protection. What joy accompanied this! What help and blessings have come from it! Frequently renewing this consecration and wearing a medal and scapular of Our Lady help to keep me mindful of her constant love and care.

Though many outside the Catholic Church (and a good number within) struggle with devotion to her (as I did), Mary is proving in many quarters to be more of a bridge than a barrier in ecumenical relations. The Orthodox Church, though separated from Catholic unity in the eleventh century, has always retained a great devotion to Our Lady; it seems to even be stronger than that of many practicing Catholics in the United States who have either abandoned or neglected devotion to her. Muslims too have a great reverence for Mary. There are more references to her in the Koran than in the Bible! There is also an amazing new interest in Marian devotion among our Protestant brothers and sisters. Many Christians of various denominations have been discovering anew the special role and place of Mary for us today. Examples of this are the Anglican theologian John Macquarrie's Mary for All Christians; the book on Mary by Max Thurian, as a Calvinist; the Methodist minister's Five for Sorrow, Ten for Joy, on the mysteries of the rosary and Pentecostal minister Jerry Sandidge's paper entitled "A Pentecostal Perspective of Mary," presented at the 1981 Roman Catholic/Pentecostal Dialogue. Rather than a cause of division among Christians, Mary can be for us a source of unity. She is Mother of us all. What's in a mother's heart if not the prayer that her family, her children be together?

That she and all the saints in heaven can pray for us, is a teaching of the Catholic Church — affirmed again at the Second Vatican Council. [2] It's part of what has been believed from early times as expressed in the Apostles Creed about "the communion of saints". These brothers and sisters of ours, this "cloud of witnesses" (Heb 12:1), don't forget us once they get to the goal but urge us on by their example and their prayers. We can be in a wonderful "communion" with them as life goes along. They are part of the family of the Church — the Church triumphant. They, with the angels, are our special friends and companions, particularly our guardian angel and our patron saint. Queen of them all, however, is Mary.

The book of Revelations speaks about those who "stand before God's throne and worship him day and night in his temple" (Rev 7:15). They sing God's praises (v. 10) and "the prayers of all the holy ones" rise like incense before the Lord (Rev 8:3-4). Their prayers can be offered for us and she who interceded with her Son at the marriage feast of Cana (Jn 2:1-11) still intercedes for us in our needs.

If you're Catholic and you've wandered away from the family of the Church or are tempted to do so—think of Mary and regularly ask her prayers. You can do the same if you are not Catholic. *My experience and that of countless others is that she helps to draw us closer to Jesus, His Church and all our brothers and sisters in the human family. She is Mother of God, Mother of the Church and Queen of Peace.*

GIFT OF THE CHURCH

Chapter 11

THE EUCHARIST JUST SYMBOLIC OR FOR REAL?

"This *is* my body . . . This *is* my blood"
(Mt 26:26-28/ Mk 14:22-24/Lk 22:19-20)

During the first parish mission I gave at the end of the sabbatical, a man shared this witness. He said that for ten years he left the Catholic Church, attended many other different churches, and tried to hate the Church. But eventually God brought him back. He attributed it especially to two realities: the Holy Eucharist and Our Lady. "In all those years," he said, "in all the different churches I attended, I never found the same reverence, attention to and deep belief in the real presence of Christ in this sacrament as I found in the Catholic Church. And besides that, in all those years, I kept a rosary in my pocket. I don't know why I did it. It didn't make sense. But I couldn't get rid of it — and I believe she brought me home again."

Together with true devotion to Mary, the Eucharist (a lawful and valid keeping of the Lord Jesus' sacrifice and supper, with the belief in the real and not just symbolic presence of Jesus Christ, Body and Blood, soul and divinity in the sacrament of the altar) is a hallmark of the true Church. It is also a powerful means of unity and healing, reconciliation and spiritual renewal.

The Scriptures are clear enough about Jesus' intention regarding the Eucharist. St. Paul gives the earliest written account in the New Testament of the institution of the Lord's supper. "For I received from the Lord what I also handed on to you, that the Lord Jesus, on the night he was handed over, took bread, and, after he had given thanks, broke it and said, 'This is my body that is for you. Do this in remembrance of me.' In the same way also the cup, after supper, saying, 'This cup is the new covenant in my blood. Do this, as often as you drink it, in remembrance of me.'" Paul goes on to show the sacrificial aspect of this action: "For as often as you eat this bread and drink the cup, you proclaim the death of the Lord until he comes." Then he adds: "Therefore, whoever eats the bread or drinks the cup of the Lord unworthily will have to answer for the body and blood of the Lord" (1 Cor 11:23-27). All three synoptic Gospels also give the account of the last supper and the words of Our Lord "This is my body . . . This is my blood."

John, the author of the fourth Gospel, who wrote after all the others and in whose day the practice of celebrating the Eucharist (or Mass as we call it now) was common, does not repeat again the account of the institution. In his sixth chapter, however, he presents a moving discourse of Our Lord about Himself as "the bread of life," the new "manna" for our earthly journey. "Amen, amen, I say to you, unless you eat the flesh of the Son of Man and drink his blood, you do not have life within you. Whoever eats my flesh and drinks my blood has eternal life, and I will raise him on the last day. For my flesh is true food, and my blood is true drink. Whoever eats my flesh and drinks my blood remains in me and I in him" (v. 53-56).

The Bible leaves little doubt that what Jesus is giving us is truly but mysteriously His Flesh to eat and His Blood to drink. What Hippolytus, a priest and Father of the Church who lived in the 2nd century after Jesus, says about scriptural interpretation in general certainly applies to the Eucharistic texts. "Sacred Scripture is God's gift to us, and it should be understood in the way that He intends; we should not do violence to it by interpreting it according to our own preconceived ideas". [1] That the early Church interpreted the words of Jesus to mean just what He was saying is clear from numerous writings of the Fathers of the Church, from evidence in the catacombs and elsewhere and from a constant practice and teaching of the Church down through the ages.

What makes people stumble is the same thing that made the first listeners (in John's account) stumble. "This saying is hard, who can accept it?" (6:60). It boggles our minds so *naturally* we reject it. That's why we need the *supernatural* grace of faith. "The words I have spoken to you are spirit and life" (v. 63). They can only be accepted through an openness to and action of the Holy Spirit.

I still remember vividly the African-American minister who appeared with me before a religion class of teenagers of different Christian faiths. Two Protestant ministers and I were asked to each give a brief explanation of our Sunday worship. Of course, I spoke about the Mass. Among other things I said that it is our Catholic faith that at the moment of consecration when the priest pronounces the words

"This is my body . . . This is my blood" truly and not just symbolically the bread and wine are substantially changed into the Body and Blood of the Lord. I added something like "Now I can't speak for my brother clergymen here today, but I do know that outside of the Catholic Church there are many Christians who believe that the Holy Eucharist is only a symbol and not actually the Body and Blood of Jesus Christ." Then this minister spoke. What he said I don't think I'll ever forget.

"I too can't speak for my brother minister here," he began, "but I'll tell you what I believe. I believe that it is the Body of Our Lord Jesus Christ. You ask me how to explain that," he continued, "and I answer I can't explain it. But when I pick up the Bible and I read the prologue of St. John's Gospel in which he says 'The Word was made flesh and dwelt among us' — I can't explain that. But if I can believe that the eternal Son of God, equal to the Father in power and majesty, took our flesh and became like one of us — then I can believe that He can take a piece of bread and change it into His Body! I also know that when I die my body will be buried in the ground and turn back into dust, but I believe that on the last day God will give me a new body in the glorious resurrection. If I can believe that — I can believe that Jesus Christ can change bread into His Body!"

For many ages this mystery has been expressed in Catholic theology and Church pronouncements by the word "transubstantiation" - a change of one substance into another. Every created thing is made up of substance and accidents, or in popular language, of an inner reality or essence and outward appearances. *Transubstantiation* simply means that the substance of bread and wine is changed into the substance of the Body and Blood of Our Lord while the accidents or appearances remain the same.

I would put it this way. What we can do by human power is to change many of the appearances of things while their substance or essence or inner reality remains the same. I can take a book, for example, and dip it in a vat of liquid chocolate and then let it dry. It would end up looking like a big chocolate bar but inwardly and essentially it would still remain a book. What God can do is to take anything He made and *change the inner reality* while allowing all the outward appearances to remain the same. This is what He does in the Holy Eucharist. By the power of His word, we are no longer dealing with bread essentially or substantially but with the Body of Christ. All the appearances remain but the substance of bread has been changed into the substance of Jesus Christ, the God-man, the risen Lord.

The early Church Fathers consistently express the truth of the real and not just symbolic presence of Jesus in the Eucharist. For help in reviewing their multitudinous statements regarding this and other doctrines of Catholic faith, I would again recommend Jurgens' book The Faith of the Early Fathers with its doctrinal index. Among other statements on the subject, in his letters (on the way to martyrdom ca. 110), Ignatius warns against those who follow false teachings and says, "They abstain from the Eucharist and from prayer, because they do not confess that *the Eucharist is the Flesh of Our Savior Jesus Christ, Flesh which suffered for our sins and which the Father, in His goodness, raised up again*. They who deny the gift of God are perishing in their disputes." 2

Justin, another martyr and early Church Father, whose life spans a period from around the year 100 to 165 A.D., describes in some detail the structure of the Mass in his day, much like ours today. About Holy Communion he writes "We call this food Eucharist; and no one else is permitted to partake of it, except one who believes our teaching to be true and who has been washed in the washing which is for the remission of sins and for regeneration, and is thereby living as Christ has enjoined. For not as common bread nor common drink do we receive these; but since Jesus Christ our Savior was made incarnate by the word of God and had both flesh and blood for our salvation, so too, as we have been taught, *the food which has been made into the Eucharist* by the Eucharistic prayer set down by Him, and by the change of which our blood and flesh is nourished, *is both the flesh and the blood of that incarnated Jesus"*. [3]

While many non-Catholic Christians have begun to accept this truth, it is a great tragedy that many modern Catholic Christians have abandoned or never been made fully aware of it. A recent Gallup poll among Catholics in the U.S. claims that a majority of them subscribe to a merely symbolic understanding of the sacrament or the erroneous position that He is present only if you believe He is. Some have taken up the old Lutheran position that bread and wine are unchanged but that Jesus is none the less present. Amazingly, another recent poll reveals that more Lutherans in our country now have the Catholic view of the Holy Eucharist than American Catholics![4] What some Catholics have sadly lost — some Protestants have gladly found!

One of the most frequently quoted texts from the document on the liturgy of the 2nd Vatican Council is "Christ is always present in His Church...not only in the person of His minister (the priest) ... but especially under the Eucharistic species ... in His word, since it is He Himself who speaks when the holy Scriptures are read in the Church. He is present, finally, when the Church prays and sings, for He promised: 'Where two or three are gathered together in my name, there am I in the midst of them'" (Mt 18:20).5

When the text is freely quoted, however, the speaker often misses the very important word "*especially*" which precedes "under the Eucharistic species". We truly can meet Jesus in all the ways mentioned in this text—the gathering together, the Word, the priest—but we meet Him *especially* in the consecrated bread and wine. He is present in all the other ways but especially and uniquely present in this way. *He is present in all the other ways, but He is substantially present with His Body and Blood only in the Holy Eucharist.*

According to full Catholic understanding, for the Eucharist to be valid it must be celebrated by a validly ordained bishop or priest and according to at least the most basic and essential matter and form of celebration approved by the Church. Celebrating a valid Eucharist is at the heart of Christian worship and a sign and cause of the true Church of Our Lord Jesus Christ. *Thank God that in modern times the Holy Spirit is bringing Christians of different denominations closer together in their understanding and appreciation of the mystery of the altar, both regarding the real bodily presence and the Eucharist as a sacrifice.*

This is evident not only from the Anglican and Roman Catholic dialogue but also in the Lutheran-Catholic consultation where, for example, it is stated: "We affirm that in the sacrament of the Lord's supper, Jesus Christ, true God and true man, is present wholly and entirely, in His body and blood, under the signs of bread and wine." [6] From the other side of the Reformation (the Presbyterians and Reformed) the same truth is expressed: "The real presence of Christ in the Eucharist . . . *does not depend upon the belief of each individual, but on the power of Christ's Word* . . . and upon His promise to bind Himself to the sacramental event as a sign of His person given to us." [7]

There are other Christian bodies as well that have expressed similar views on the subject. All of this does not mean that complete agreement has been reached regarding all aspects of Eucharistic doctrine. But it does mean that we've come a long way in the area of agreement about a sacrament and sacrifice that is a hallmark of the true Church. *That the Catholic Church throughout her two thousand years has never wavered in her unambiguous official proclamation of this truth of faith is another sign of her being the true Church of Our Lord Jesus Christ.*

The real change of bread and wine in the Eucharist is meant to bring about a *real change* in us who receive Him. When I began that sabbatical of 1982, I attended a week of lectures sponsored by the continuing education program of our diocese at a center across the lake from New Orleans. When the course ended, I drove back into the city to a Mass that was celebrating a ten-year anniversary of a charismatic prayer group at St. Gabriel's parish. I remember vividly that evening the feelings I had as I drove across that long Lake Pontchartrain Causeway bridge. I could only compare it with the way a man must feel when a good wife and children have just walked out on him.

I had, a week before, just left my last parish family and knew I wasn't going back to them or to any parish because of the new work I was preparing to undertake. Inside my heart there was a feeling of darkness, emptiness and sadness. As I took part in the Mass that night the feeling was still with me; but when the time of Holy Communion came what happened was unforgettable. As Jesus came to me in this sacrament — He who knew exactly how I felt — He entered the darkness with His light, the sadness with His joy, the emptiness with His fullness and He lifted me right up! Certainly I don't expect this emotionally every time I receive Holy Communion, but what I am now more aware of is this. Every time He comes, He comes to me *just as I am*. He knows exactly what I need. And He comes, whether I feel it or not, to supply my deepest needs, especially my spiritual needs.

That experience at the Eucharist, together with another during the sabbatical which involved a healing of a very hurtful memory, helped to make me more aware of the power of Jesus in this sacrament to transform us — body, mind, emotions, memories, and especially our inner spirit. When we eat other bread, it is changed into us; when we eat this bread, we are little by little changed into Him! He is truly "the resurrection and the life" (Jn 11:25) and proclaims that "the one who feeds on me will have life because of me" (Jn 6:57). Besides these and other personal experiences, I've heard and read many witnesses of what happened to people physically, mentally, and spiritually through the Eucharist.

What is needed on the part of all is a lively faith in the mystery of Christ's real presence in this sacrament and a great expectancy of and cooperation with what He wants to do in us each time we attend Mass and approach the table of the Lord. He wants to transform us individually but also as a community, breaking down barriers of resentment and pride, lack of communication and love. "Because the loaf of bread is one, we, though many, are one body, for we all partake of the one loaf" (1 Cor 10:17). With each Eucharist we're called to an ever deeper incorporation into Christ and His body, the Church. The primary effect of this sacrament is meant to be growth in unity and love.

A number of years ago I attended an ecumenical seminar at Emory University in Atlanta on the subject of Christian preaching. There were speakers and participants representing many different denominations. One was a dynamic young African-American minister, a professor at a theological college, who delivered a stirring, soul-filled sermon as an example of preaching in the Pentecostal churches. Afterwards a priest friend of mine, who was also attending the conference, had lunch with him. He told the minister how impressed he was with his sermon and how he thought we Catholics needed more of that kind of enthusiasm and liveliness in our preaching and worship. His response was something like this. "Yes Father, I agree with you. You do need that, and I see it coming more and more in the Catholic Church. But let me tell you something. I've gone to Mass from time to time in a Catholic church, and I've watched the priest closely at the altar. I've noticed how, after Holy Communion, he so carefully gathers up every little crumb that's left over and so thoroughly cleanses the chalice so that not even one drop of the wine remains. I've said to myself 'Wow! these people really believe that this is the Body and Blood of the Lord Jesus!' *If you could get across to your congregation and to others what you really believe — they would be breaking the doors down to get in!*"

So when they say, "I don't get anything out of the Mass", the message hasn't yet gotten across or been accepted. There is also something else that's wrong. It's not just that we priests need to offer Mass with reverence and devotion, give good homilies and help our congregations to participate. But all of God's people need to *approach the Mass not primarily for what we're going to get out of it but for what we're going to put into it.* The Mass is meant to be the supreme act of self-forgetful worship of God. Christ is unfailingly present and active in the Eucharist. How much we get out of it, however, is in proportion to what we put into it: prayer and song from the heart, attentive listening to God's word, active and lively participation, expectant faith and wholehearted surrender of ourselves with Jesus to the Father — with each Mass, more and more "letting go and letting God" take over. I would add to this the importance also of taking time after Communion (and Mass) to be aware of Jesus continuing to do His healing and saving work in us. In that spirit, we can come to experience the liturgy of the Church and especially the Eucharist, as the Second Vatican Council speaks of it, as "the summit towards which the activity of the Church is directed . . . [and] the fountain from which all her power flows!" [8]

Chapter 12

THE POPE AND THE CHURCH

"Where Peter is — **there** is the Church!"

Never in my lifetime, including over forty years as a priest, have I ever seen so many people who disconnect Jesus from His Church. "I'm all for Jesus," they say, "but the Church, forget it. Those hypocrites! I can do without it." Or it may be, "I'll find a church where I feel comfortable" or "where I'm fed" or even "I'll start my own!" *Someone who says, "I'm accepting Jesus, but not His Church" — is not truly accepting the Jesus whom God sent or God's plan of salvation in Jesus Christ. God's plan did not stop with Jesus and His ascension into heaven. That's just the beginning of the story. The rest of the story is what Jesus continues to do through His body, the Church.*

St. Luke the Evangelist clearly expresses this. After he finished his Gospel about our Lord's ministry among us through His own physical visible presence, St. Luke penned the Acts of the Apostles, which is the continuation of that ministry through His body the Church. *To accept Jesus fully is to accept the Word made flesh and the Word Who continues to enflesh Himself as it were in the visible sign of His Church. In that Church, Peter and his successors have a crucial role.*

Communists like those in Vietnam and Red China have clearly recognized this as shown by their efforts to separate the Catholic body of believers from their visible head and create a National or Peoples' Church. Those who have courageously resisted this charade have suffered greatly. The Church's enemies perceive that a way to successfully defeat or control the Catholic Church is to strike at its head or alienate the members of the Church from loyalty to him. As in the Book of Genesis to "strike at your head" is the way to defeat your enemy (3:15).

Though possibly far-fetched, in our own country there are rumblings at times of one day separating the Church in the U.S. from Rome and establishing an "American Church". Modeled on the political independence from England declared in '76, some see this as a giant step towards freedom. In actuality, it would be a giant step towards slavery! The very supra-national nature of the Church and the papacy and its universal character are in God's providence safeguards against national control and the pressure of powerful local special interest groups.

Wittingly or unwittingly the seeds of this kind of rebellion are sown by those within or outside of the Church who help set people at odds with the Pope, ridiculing his statements or actions and casting him in a bad light, lessening loyalty and respect for his guidance. Unity in the Church, however, and preservation of the integrity of Catholic faith calls for union, in the plan of God, with the rock upon whom Jesus built and continues to build His Church.

"Ubi Petrus, Ibi Ecclesia", "Where Peter is there is the Church" is an ancient expression of faith originating with St. Ambrose (339-397), an early Church Father and bishop. We've already talked about St. Peter and Jesus' plan for him and his successors. He was clearly appointed as chief shepherd of the flock (Jn 21:15-19) and main foundation stone of the building of the Church (Mt 16:18). He was also after Jesus the visible head of that Church which Paul calls "Christ's body" (1 Cor 12:27) on earth. *It follows that those who want to be fully incorporated in the flock of the Great Shepherd Jesus are called to be in the flock of His chief shepherd on earth. Those who want to be completely joined to the edifice of the Church which Christ is continuing to build must be joined to the earthly foundation and central stone of the building — to Peter and his successors. Those who want to be truly in union not only with Jesus, the head, but also with His body, the Church on earth, must be in union with the visible head of that body.*

It is true that the early Church did not have a well-worked-out theology of the role of Peter or his successors. But that's true of many other realities of our faith, including the divinity of Jesus, the Trinity, the Holy Eucharist, the sacraments, Our Lady, all the implications of Christian morality and so on down the line. Jesus told the apostles before he left them, "I have much more to tell you, but you cannot bear it now. But when he comes, the Spirit of truth, he will guide you to all truth" (Jn 16:12-13). As I've learned from my own life, God teaches more things by experience than by mere words. It was through the living out of the mission of Peter and his successors through the ages that the Church, under the guidance of the Holy Spirit, came to appreciate and understand better the role that Jesus wanted for the chief earthly shepherd of His flock.

As time goes along, it becomes clearer and clearer how much we need a central head in the Church to continue that mission of Peter and bring unity and clear teaching to a people often confused and divided. Since in this world of ours there is no one who even makes any serious claim to being that successor other than the Pope, many outside of the Catholic Church have begun to take a new look at his role and have a new understanding and appreciation of his mission in the wonderful providence and plan of God.

Even the representatives of the Orthodox and Roman Catholic Churches in 1274 at the 2nd Council of Lyons came to a common understanding and acceptance of papal primacy (and other subjects of division) and the Orthodox Church which was separated from the Catholic Church in the 11th century was once again officially united with her.[1] Though the union was shortlived, it continues to be the object of our hopes and prayers and efforts; and there are significant signs that these are bearing fruit. Catholic News Service at the beginning of 1992 quoted Bishop Pierre Duprey, secretary of the Pontifical Council for Promoting Christian Unity, as saying that the two Churches were now in "almost total communion." [2]

On my sabbatical I visited the famous ecumenical community in Taize, France — to which people of all ages, but especially young people, flock from all over the world seeking spiritual renewal, unity and peace. The permanent members of the community of Taize take vows of poverty, chastity, and obedience but belong to different Christian denominations. In that community, however, there was a very clear understanding that if we are to find unity among Christians today, we must not neglect the providential role of the Pope in bringing that unity about. Upon reception of its first Catholic member in 1969, the community worked out a text during its annual council, one section of which reads: "The simple fact of having Catholic brothers among us stimulates us to live more and more in anticipation of unity by placing ourselves in communion with the minister who is the servant of the servants of God (the Pope)." This theme figured in some of the addresses given in 1971 by Brother Roger Schultz, Protestant founder of Taize. Speaking in New York to a gathering of Episcopal bishops (Anglican Communion), he said, "Is it now still possible for us to envisage the unity of the Church without even touching on the question of the Bishop of Rome? And yet there is still a conspiracy of silence around his ministry of unity, even among certain Catholics. *Every local community needs a pastor to gather together the flock always inclined to fragment and scatter. Can we really hope to see the Church gather in unity unless it has a similar pastor for its universality*?" [3]

Historically, Anglicanism completely repudiated the authority of the Pope when it broke from the Catholic Church in the fifteen hundreds. For that reason it is all the more striking that in the final report (1981) of the dialogue of the International Commission of Anglicans and Roman Catholics (without all the questions of the role of the Pope being resolved), there emerged a united acceptance of the need for a central authority in a reunited Church. *"We nevertheless agree that a universal primacy will be needed in a reunited Church and should appropriately be the primacy of the Bishop of Rome . . . In a reunited Church a ministry modeled on the role of Peter will be a sign and safeguard of such unity."* 4

Even on the question of the teaching authority of the Church and the Pope (still without full agreement), the progress made in mutual understanding in this dialogue of Anglicans and Roman Catholics was phenomenal. "When matters of faith are at stake, decisions may be made by the Church in universal councils; we are agreed that these are authoritative. *We have also recognized that need in a united Church for a universal primate who presiding over the koinonia can speak with authority in the name of the Church. Through both these agencies, the Church can make a decisive judgment in matters of faith and so exclude error."* 5

Though there are still many forces of division among Christians, the Holy Spirit is calling the Christian denominations together in regard to doctrine and discipline and the role of Peter and his successors. *Many are coming to see in a new light the plan of God in the selection of Peter and the meaning of Ambrose's words "where Peter is — there is the Church."*

Chapter 13

LIFE AND THE ACT OF LOVE THAT LEADS TO LIFE

The Good News about birth control!

Within recent years I've heard the testimony of a brilliant former Presbyterian pastor and seminary professor who is now a Catholic. He came from a position of intense anti-Catholicism, and the first crack in the dike was the Catholic Church's position on birth control! Actually it was this, together with the Church's consistent, historical, anti-abortion and pro-life stand (when many other denominations in the 20th century began to either collapse or go silent on the subject) that began to open his wife's mind and then his to all the treasures of wisdom and knowledge offered by our Church. [1]

On the other hand, the birth control issue was a turning point in modern times for many Catholics in regard to open revolt or quiet resistance to the official teachings of the Church. I say this not just as a cool outside observer but as one who, as a pastor, personally agonized over the issue and resisted. It's just one of the many moral teachings of the

Church — all of which can be summed up in the command of Jesus to love God with your whole heart and soul and to love your neighbor as yourself (Mt 22:34-40) — but it did receive more attention (from the media as well) and was a cause of more objection and dissension than almost all the others.

Unnatural forms of birth control, however, are actually thousands of years old. They go back to centuries before the coming of Christ and have been addressed by the Church since very early times. In an ancient catechism of the Church, the Didache (ca. 140 A.D.), where there is an explicit condemnation of abortion — there seem to be implicit anti-contraceptive references as well. [2] In fact, John Noonan's classical study Contraception shows a continuous Catholic history of contraceptive condemnation. This was not only true of the pastoral and official pronouncements of the Church but of theologians as well. Noonan says that until more recent times "Never had it been admitted by a Catholic theologian that complete sexual intercourse might be had in which by deliberation, procreation was excluded." [3]

The subject gained greater public awareness in the 1960s because of the scientific development of the anovulant pill and growing questioning among many Catholics. In an effort to clarify the issue, especially about the medical and scientific aspects of the pill, Pope Paul VI sought help from a special advisory commission (which John XXIII had originally created for population study). [4]

When finally the commission submitted its report, a majority of the members wanted a change in the birth control stance of the Church while a minority maintained the traditional teaching. At this juncture it was naturally the

Pope's responsibility as chief teacher in the Church to issue a statement on the matter.

The statement, now famous (infamous to some!) is the encyclical letter "Humanae Vitae", "Of Human Life", issued July 25, 1968. In it, Pope Paul VI maintained the age old teaching of the Church, pointing out, as one modern writer puts it, that *"the advocates of contraception had failed to produce logical and theologically convincing reasons for change. Instead, their reasons introduced principles which threatened to and did create general moral havoc."* 5

Immediately there was a storm of protest on the part of many theologians in the U.S. and elsewhere; and many priests, religious, and lay people concluded that the Pope's instruction in "Humanae Vitae" did not have to (at least always) be followed. I was in that number. I wonder now how many of the dissenters just relied on the commentators and failed to even take the trouble to read objectively and in full the statement of the Pope! I'm not sure I did. Many years later when I read it calmly, I was amazed at its wisdom and compassion. I recommend it; it's not that long or complicated. It is a profound, positive statement about the plan of God and deep meaning of a man and woman's sexual relationship in marriage, into which they are called to enter lovingly and *unreservedly* — and only in that context does it condemn any unnatural use of marital intercourse. It was and still is a practice among many of us clergy, however, to avoid the subject and when asked, to unconvincingly let people know the Church's position but then to tell them that ultimately they have to make their own decisions in conscience weighing all the circumstances. *I believe that this type of guidance (or misguidance) con-*

tributed to many people making their own decisions about other teachings of the Church as well. (As I look back on it now, I wonder why I didn't say "make your own decision" or "form your conscience" about abortion or homosexual practice or grand larceny!)

I now realize that the greatest compassion and love calls us to clearly and heartily proclaim the truth, the full good news of God's plan for our lives.

Children in the sight of God and throughout the pages of the Bible are always looked upon as precious invaluable gifts of the Lord. In the Gospels of both Matthew and Mark, after Jesus calls us back to the original plan of the Creator for man and woman in marriage, He demonstrates His own open and welcoming attitude toward children and says, "Let the children come to me and do not prevent them; for the kingdom of heaven belongs to such as these" (Mk 19:14). The begetting and rearing of children and the loving union of man and woman are considered by the Church as the great purposes for which God instituted marriage in the beginning.

The Second Vatican Council singled out married couples as deserving of "special mention who ... undertake to bring up suitably even a relatively large family." 6 The same Council did, however, talk about responsible parenthood. With "Humanae Vitae", it recognized that there could be and often are legitimate reasons for limiting the size of the family. But there is a God-given way of doing it, and there is also an unnatural and immoral way. The way makes a big difference.

God created sexual relations to be enjoyed by married couples. He didn't command them to engage in it every day or every week or every month. They have the right to do so or not according to mutual agreement. But when they do have sex, they have to do so according to the will of God who made it. Natural Family Planning for avoiding pregnancy simply means limiting sexual relations to those times when, according to nature's design, conception would not take place. In the understanding of the Church, such a practice would be justified not for convenience or any selfish motive, but for substantial reasons. NFP is also used effectively by couples who want to achieve pregnancy.

When mention is made of Natural Family Planning, many people think we're still talking about calendar "rhythm". *Modern NFP has advanced as far beyond rhythm as the auto over the buggy*! The limited period every month that a woman is fertile can now be determined with great accuracy by certain bodily signs. *A government study of NFP verifies the claim that it can be 99% effective*! [7] That's as effective as all of the on-going unnatural means of birth control and more effective than some.

What is significant is that couples who make the decision of using natural rather than unnatural means of birth control certainly make a sacrifice, but one that brings untold blessings to their married life. Among these are increased communication and a new appreciation of one another, of God's wonderful creation and of sex itself. Whereas about 50% of marriages in the US break up in divorce, NFP couples rarely divorce! [8]

When the pill first came out, I was among those who thought we had struck upon a great new invention. How mistaken I was! The ill effects of the pill on many who have used it have yet to be fully revealed. I wonder, however, how many people who use the pill ever stop to read the package insert that according to government regulations of the Food and Drug Administration outlines the seemingly endless list of all the possible harmful side effects. These effects are only to be expected since *the pill dramatically disrupts the body's regular hormonal balance.*

The worst effect of the pill (and even more so of the IUD, the Depo-Provera® injection and Norplant® — under-the-skin implant) is the potential to cause abortions at a very early stage of life. All the birth control pills alter the uterine lining in such a way that it becomes hostile to the implantation of a newly fertilized egg. Even though ovulation and fertilization are usually impeded by the most commonly used pills, it does at times take place. But the changes brought about in the endometrium (lining of the uterus) *"reduce the likelihood of implantation"* (to use the words of the standard Physicians' Desk Reference). 9

Bogamir Kuhar, president of Pharmacists for Life, estimates that *there are many more early and hidden abortions caused by the pill, IUD and Norplant® than by surgical abortions*! — What all of this says to me: How important and prophetic is the anti-contraceptive teaching of the Church! It not only protects sexuality in marriage but even human life as well!

It was a presentation at the beginning of that sabbatical of 1982 on the ill effects of the pill and other contraceptives contrasted with the beneficial effects of NFP that began to alter my thinking about this whole issue. All the physical and psychological side effects were to me like a red light warning — nature screaming out "Something's wrong!" Nature is also calling out about NFP: "Something's right!"

But what's the deepest reason why unnatural birth control is morally wrong? Basically because sex is God's creation ("from the beginning the Creator 'made them male and female'" [Mt 19:4]), and it needs to be used the way He intended. *In sharing with us the power to give life, He joined it to an intimate expression of self-giving love. To unnaturally separate the act of love from its possible life-giving effect is to tamper with and seriously violate a sacred gift of God.* When nature provides non-fertile periods, it's God's work; when we create them against nature's plan in order to circumvent that plan, we go against God's will.

Let me give an example. Let's say you sit down to eat a delicious meal, but before doing so you put a tube in your throat to catch the food so you could still get the taste of eating and the socializing that may go with it. But then you take the tube after you're finished and throw it in the garbage can. What's the difference between that and the use of condoms, diaphragms, foams, pills, oral or anal sex, mutual masturbation and all the rest? All are designed one way or the other to block, destroy, or interfere with the natural effect of the marriage act. The pleasure of the act is achieved to an extent but the life-giving effect intended by the Creator is unnaturally frustrated. The difference between this and NFP is that in the case of Natural Family Planning the couple is not *abusing* but *using* nature. They do not interfere with a sacred God-designed process but by self-control make use of the natural rhythm of fertile and non-fertile days as designed by the Creator.

Another way of looking at it that is less graphic and more subtle is this: *Sexual intercourse is meant to express the total gift of oneself to another without anything being held back.* It should even "by objective standards . . . preserve the full sense of mutual self-giving and human procreation in the context of true love" (Vatican II).[10] It is intended by God to be an expression and renewal of the marriage agreement and covenant. It should be saying again, "I take you and give myself to you for better or worse, for richer or for poorer, in sickness and in health, without any conditions, until death." *In the use of contraceptives of any kind, a couple is not saying this unreservedly. There is a hidden agenda, a holding back, a conditional consent: "I am giving myself to you but not completely."*

The marital union, modeled on the union of Christ and His Church, is a call to total unselfish self-giving and holiness. "Husbands, love your wives, even as Christ loved the Church and handed himself over for her to sanctify her..." (Eph 5:25-26). Unnaturally blocking off fertility (an integral part of who a person is) in the very act of marriage always contradicts the complete self donation and holiness (wholeness) of the act.

What is said above would also (and even more so) apply to permanent sterilization for the purpose of birth control, carrying with it the added evil of unjustified bodily mutilation. The more than one million a year sterilizations in the US are not without their own harmful side effects, both physically and psychologically. [11]

Do you know that before 1930 all the Christian denominations were in agreement about the evil of artificial birth control? Protestant denominations stood shoulder to shoulder with the Catholic Church on the subject for about 400 years. It was in 1930, however, that one denomination, the Anglican bishops at their Lambeth Conference in England, reluctantly made some exceptions in the birth control issue. Twice before in the 1900s the Lambeth Conference had unequivocally condemned artificial birth control. Does it suddenly become all right in 1930?

The Anglican break was soon echoed in the U.S.. In March of 1931, the majority of a committee of the U.S. Federal Council of Churches (a forerunner of today's National Council of Churches) endorsed "the careful and restrained use of contraceptives by married people." 12 The immediate reaction to this was outrage on the part of many Protestant leaders. But as time went on, more and more got on the band wagon (and some of the denominations which began by accepting contraception then moved on to the acceptance of other deviant sexual behavior and abortion as well). A hole had been made in the dike and the wall began to crumble. Thank God, the Catholic Church has not gone along with the tide. What it says today is consistent with what it said yesterday and the day before and for almost 2,000 years. Thank God that the Church especially in the person of its earthly head, the successor of St. Peter, can stand tall in the world and still speak a clear unequivocal word and say that sex, including sex in marriage, has to be used according to the will and plan of the Creator, and that unnatural separation of its unitive and life-giving purposes is immoral.

When the Pope was getting ready to visit our country some years ago, the media commentators and reporters interviewed many Catholics and took polls among us specifically regarding this issue, as well as a number of related issues. How many of you, they asked, believe that abortion is wrong? How many believe that premarital sex or homosexual practices are wrong? How many believe that artificial birth control in marriage is wrong?

It was amazing how many Catholics said they thought these acts were not wrong. Well, how do we find out what's right and wrong in this area — and in many other areas of life? Do we keep taking polls every year to see what the majority has to say and then go along with the majority? If that's the way, then morality would change from year to year or at least from decade to decade. Is that the way Jesus left us to find out right and wrong? If it were, then we'd be in a mess! *And that's why we're in a mess*! Many of us just go along with what the current thinking seems to be or with what we think it ought to be. But, thank God, that's not the way He meant it to be. He didn't just go away to heaven and say, "Well, boys and girls, you figure it out for yourselves." No — he left us a Church with the authority to teach us and show us the way.

Even some of the opponents of the Church's position have had to admit as Pope Paul warned in his encyclical that if the door were open to contraception in marriage there would no longer be adequate reason to object to other forms of abberant sexual behavior. For example, Michael F. Valente years ago clearly identified himself as a dissenter from "Humanae Vitae" in his book, <u>Sex, The Radical View of a Catholic Theologian</u>. Yet Valente admitted that "It seems unreasonable to maintain that there is a difference between allowing a husband and wife to use the condom and allowing them to have anal intercourse since neither fulfills the natural law doctrine's requirement of insemination in the vagina. Likewise, there is no difference between using the condom and coitus interruptus (withdrawal), or any of the other so called sins prohibited under the doctrine such as masturbation, homosexuality and bestiality (intercourse with animals)." [13] I don't know of any writer who has seriously tried to prove Valente wrong. In addition to all this, as the Pope also predicted, easy access to contraceptives has increased premarital sex, as well as marital infidelity and break-ups, and contributed to a lessening of respect for women.

There is also evidence that *the widespread use of contraceptives has not decreased the number of abortions* (as at one time I thought it would) *but that it has dramatically increased them*. Fr. Paul Marx O.S.B. who for years has been traveling the earth in behalf of "Human Life International" testifies to this and so does Fr. Lee Kaylor, the youthful San Francisco priest who is founder of the pro-life organization called "Priests For Life." Most abortions, he says, "are simply contraceptive back—ups." A recent pro-contraceptive article in a popular health magazine stated, "According to the Alan Guttmacher Institute, a leading think tank for population research, as many as half of all women who have abortions were using birth control when they got pregnant." [14]

Though the Pope did not say that his particular encyclical "Of Human Life" was intended to be infallible, there are serious reasons for considering the anti-contraceptive position of the Church infallible by virtue of the universal and long—standing way in which it has been proclaimed. [15] The Popes of this century, one after the other, as well as the world Synod of bishops on the Family in 1980, have reaffirmed this constant teaching.

In any case, the Church does not always have to make infallible pronouncements to speak with the authority Jesus gave her. "Go, therefore, and make disciples of all nations," He said (Mt 28:19). "Whoever listens to you, listens to me" (Lk 10:16). And Paul urges Timothy: "proclaim the word;

be persistent whether it's convenient or inconvenient" (2 Tim 4:2). Preaching on contraception has always been unpopular. St. Jerome complained about this reaction to the subject in the 4th century.

The desire to be accepted or popular is a constant trap for most human beings, including many of us preachers and pastors. I think it's a special curse of our age. The Church of Christ, however, like her Founder and invisible Head, is meant to be counter-cultural, "a sign that will be contradicted" (Lk 2:34), always challenging us, "Do not conform yourself to this age but be transformed by the renewal of your mind . . ." (Rom 12:2).

The fact that so many people disagree is no sign that the teaching Church is wrong. On the contrary, it could well be another sign that she is right. How many, for example, if you had taken a poll, would have agreed with the social justice teachings of the Church at the time they were promulgated?

The Catholic Church's position (like all of her moral teachings) is based upon an understanding of natural law, the law of human nature as created by God; but it also, like the other teachings, ***has its roots in tradition and in Sacred Scripture***. Besides the passages already quoted, we could cite those regarding the severe condemnation of unnatural acts with persons of the same sex and with animals. In the Old Testament such acts were punishable by death (Lev 20:13 & 15). In the New Testament they are singled out as examples of how low men and women can fall when they reject or neglect God (Rom 1:22-28). These texts, by implication, would also censure all unnatural use of sex. The most famous passage, however, that refers specifically to an act of unnatural birth prevention is in Genesis, Chapter 38, verses 9-10.

According to an ancient Near Eastern custom (later called the levirate law), if a married man died childless, his brother was obliged to take the widow as his wife and sire children in his brother's name. Onan married Tamar, widow of his deceased brother, but regularly practiced the most ancient form of prevention, withdrawal. "Whenever he had relations with his brother's widow, he wasted his seed on the ground, to avoid contributing offspring for his brother. What he did greatly offended the Lord, and the Lord took his life too" (Gen 38:9-10). For generations the sin of artificial birth control was called by Christians "onanism" because of their consistent understanding of this passage as a condemnation of all unnatural forms of prevention.

In the 20th century, however, there has been a shift from what had been an almost universal Christian interpretation of the passage. Many scholars now say the penalty for Onan's action was due not to the *how* of what he did but to the *why. There is serious reason to wonder, however, how much this new interpretation is influenced by a changing morality and the premise that birth control is not that bad.*

Certainly the main point of the story is that Onan did not fulfill his duty as brother-in-law to raise up offspring but this itself would not incur the severe condemnation of death. The Bible in Deut 25:7-10 clearly spells out the penalty for violating the levirate requirement; it is public disgrace, not capital punishment. Onan's severe penalty points to something special about what he did.

The older scholars both Catholic [16] and Protestant [17] surely knew about the levirate law but they saw in the text more than just that. To them it included a condemnation of Onan's unnatural contraceptive behavior. It is also noteworthy that "The Jewish interpretation contemporary with early Christianity taught that in Genesis 38 coitus interruptus (withdrawal) was condemned by God." [18]

Manuel Miguens, a modern Scripture scholar, who does not go along with the new interpretation, points out that the translation, "he wasted his seed on the ground" fails to do full justice to the Hebrew expression, *shichet*. The verb never means simply to waste or spill; it means to spoil or ruin, to corrupt or pervert. "... His perversion or corruption consists in his action itself, not precisely in the result and goal of his act." [19]

A balanced interpretation of the text would include Onan's condemnation both for what he did and why he did it. Such is the approach in the scholarly work, <u>A New Catholic Commentary on Holy Scripture</u>, where it is stated, *"Onan's sin consisted both in his mean disregard of family duty and in the unnatural means which he used to avoid this duty."* [20] <u>Matthew Henry's Commentary</u>, a popular and widely used Protestant work puts it this way: "Onan, though he consented to marry the widow, yet, *to the great abuse of his own body, of the wife that he had married* and the memory of his brother that was gone, refused to raise up seed unto his brother." [21]

The Catholic Church's teaching is based on much more than one text however. It is based on the reading of God's law as written in the very nature of sex and marriage, on a number of biblical passages that illustrate this, and on a constant Christian tradition. The teaching is that unnatural forms of birth control in marriage are always seriously perverted acts and objectively grave sins.

With the passage of time, more and more non-Catholic leaders are returning to a position of opposition to unnatural birth control. Lutheran minister Larry Christenson and his wife, Nordis, take such a stand in their book, The Christian Couple. [22] They devote an entire chapter to the issue. An evangelical, Charles Provan, has more recently published a 100 page book called The Bible and Birth Control. [23] In it, he lists arguments just from Scripture for why artificial birth control is wrong and 99 Protestant theologians who, over a period of 400 years, took such a stand along with Catholics. Among them are Martin Luther, John Calvin and John Wesley, fathers of Protestantism.

Rev. David Prentis of the Church of Scotland in an open letter to his fellow ministers writes this: *"'Humanae Vitae' was a courageous document, going against the whole stream of opinion of its time. It was also prophetic; its predictions about the consequences of the widespread use of contraceptives proved to be woefully true. This is gradually being realized by previous opponents of 'Humanae Vitae', so that we can expect progressively a positive reappraisal of it at least in the churches.... It is to be hoped that through reflection on the damage done by contraception and the witness of the healthy marriages of those using Natural Family Planning, there will be a meeting of the minds once more."* [24]

The Catholic Church's teaching on respect for life and the act of love that leads to life is her glory. It is also among her great contributions to restoring marriage and the family, as well as respect for human sexuality and all human rights — of which the right to life is fundamental. To me — it's a mark of the true Church.

*****

Because of the many questions this particular subject raises, I've added an appendix, including usually unpublicized medical data on the harmful abortive potential of birth control drugs and devices, more information about Natural Family Planning and a list of sources.

Chapter 14

THE MESSAGE OF
THE CRUCIFIX

"We proclaim Christ *crucified*" (1 Cor 1:23)

"The message of the cross is foolishness to those who are perishing, but to us who are being saved it is the power of God. ... For Jews demand signs and Greeks look for wisdom, but we proclaim Christ crucified, a stumbling block to Jews and foolishness to Gentiles, but to those who are called, Jews and Greeks alike, Christ the power of God and the wisdom of God" (1 Cor 1:18 & 22-24).

Just as you can't talk about Jesus without talking about the cross, so you can't talk about the Catholic Church without talking about the cross. The cross, more particularly, the crucifix — the cross with Christ on it — is a very familiar symbol for Catholic people. Together with the sign of the cross traced on oneself, it's a Catholic trademark. It's everywhere — in churches, schools, Catholic office buildings, etc.

You might have heard the story of the little Jewish boy who had trouble in school with discipline. He got thrown out of one school after the other. In desperation, his parents sent him to a Catholic school. His mother couldn't wait to see if he'd even make it through one day. But finally, the school day over, little Abie came home. He was meek as a lamb! He didn't have a thing to say until eventually his mother, not able to contain herself any longer, blurted out: "What is it, Abie? We send you to all kinds of expensive schools; you act up; you get thrown out. Now we send you to a Catholic school and you come home meek as a lamb! Why? What was different?" "Well, Ma," the little boy said, "when I sat down in that classroom and looked up at the wall in front of me and saw that boy hanging on a cross, I knew they meant business in this school!"

The crucifix is the great symbol that God means business! He means business when He says, "I love you", for sacrifice is the great proof of love. He means business when He says that sin is serious business because it was sin, mine and yours, that put Him on the cross. And He means business when He says to you and me, "If anyone wishes to come after me, he must deny himself and take up his cross daily and follow me" (Lk 9:23).

The psychiatrist M. Scott Peck begins his best-seller book The Road Less Traveled with the words "Life is difficult." Everybody's life is difficult. We get in trouble when we try to skirt around the difficulties or escape from them with the misuse of drugs or alcohol or sex or excesses or wrongdoing of any kind. But when we face the difficulties and accept them and "walk through" them, we can live with peace and happiness. "Take up your cross daily and follow me" means to embrace and live fully day by day, according to God's will for you, your life, your vocation, your responsibilities. It's to take the rough and narrow road less traveled but the one "that leads to life" now and forever (Mt 7:13-14).

During my sabbatical, I made that long anticipated trip with the gospel choir of my former parish to different parts of France. It was the fulfillment of a dream for them and for me. It was an exciting and thrilling experience. I was happy and proud to be along, to be the spiritual director, and to have had a part in making that dream come true.

Somewhere along the line, however, everything began to go wrong, and I was in the middle of it and ended up being blamed for it. I remember vividly walking by myself along the French seashore one evening, with the whole impact of this seemingly awful situation crowding in on me, feeling very much alone; but I remember also that it was during that walk that I had an experience of the presence, the peace, and the strength of Our Lord in a very special way. Other props had been taken away, and I was relying on Him alone.

This experience, so much in contrast to the exuberance of the rest of the trip, helped me to reflect on the meaning of all the experiences of disappointment, pain, dryness, loss, and sorrow in my life. Why all of this? What purpose does it have? How does it fit in?

I've come to see these experiences as experiences of the cross — experiences of sharing in the mystery of the dying and rising of Jesus. *I've come to understand them,* in a way I've heard our Archbishop Schulte express it, *not as peripheral to the Christian life but as central, not as intrusions but necessary, not as accidental but providential.* I'm coming to value them, to see the hand of God in them and even — to be able to say thanks (sometimes, anyway!) in the midst of them — thanks for the experience of the cross!

Gift of the Church

Specifically, I've come to value the cross as *a purifier, a teacher*, and *a means of salvation*. Someone has said, "The purpose of life is not to satisfy but to purify." *The cross is a purifier.* Jesus says, "I am the true vine, and my Father is the vine grower. He takes away every branch in me that does not bear fruit, and everyone that does he prunes so that it bears more fruit" (Jn 15:1-2). (It's in the light of this that I understand Purgatory; it's the purification still required, if not completed by the time we die.) In the bitterness of that sabbatical experience, I was being pruned of some of my pride and reliance on human props and approval and learning to rely on Him and His approval and support.

Over and over He's offered me these opportunities to be purified. How often I've missed them! But when I have accepted them, what a blessing they have been! For example, years ago, carrying out the decision to spend a daily hour with the Lord in prayer was initially one of the hardest things I had to do. It was like pinning myself down, taming a wild stallion. It was an experience of purification. As the years have moved on, it has proved to be, with the Mass, the great means of daily renewal, strength, direction, life and joy — and I've found the need to add another hour at a later part of the day. Whereas in the beginning (and sometimes even now!) I struggled with the thought that I was wasting time and had more important things to do, I realize much more clearly than before that I'm actually choosing the *more* important thing, "the better part", as Jesus called it (Lk 10:42). Everything else seems to go better, quicker and more effectively when I give that time to the Lord in prayer. Kathryn Kuhlman, the famous woman healer and preacher, made the statement that as she looked back over her life, the

140

mountaintops and valleys, she could see the hand of God especially in the valleys. I can say the same. It was in the tough and difficult things that He was doing His most important work.

The cross is a teacher. Comparing the rearing and discipline of parents to the Father's care for us, the Letter to the Hebrews says, "They disciplined us for a short time as seemed right to them, but he does so for our benefit, in order that we may share his holiness" (Heb 12:10). The only way some of us hardheads learn is in the school of hard knocks. I remember the time I got three traffic tickets in a row for driving too fast! I had to appear in court before the judge's bench in view of a lot of people, with my Roman collar, and plead guilty before paying the fine. The embarrassment helped to get it through to me: "Hey man, you're going too fast — not just in driving but in everything! Slow down. Accept your limitations. Don't overdo." I'm still learning and haven't completely gotten the message yet, but the embarrassment was a teacher.

I realize now that whenever some painful experience comes my way, one thing I can do with it is to ask: "Lord, are you trying to tell me something?" It was through the years of restlessness and searching, of heart hunger and thirst that He taught and led me to drink more deeply from the well that never runs dry — the personal knowledge and love of Jesus Christ Himself. It was also years later through the experience, during my first pastorate, of my own limitations and failure that He brought me to my knees to ask for a power beyond my own — the outpouring of God's Holy Spirit.

I have a friend (a football-player-looking kind of guy) who's been through a bout with cancer. One day, after he had been so diagnosed, he and his wife called me over to pray with them. What he shared was something like this: "You know, before I got cancer, I never thought I needed anybody. I thought I could handle things by myself. I didn't ask others to help me, and I didn't reach out that much to others. But when I got sick, I was amazed at the number of people who reached out to me with prayer, encouraging words, offers to help; and I was ready to welcome it and ask for it. Through it all I learned that others also need me and now I'm ready to reach out to them. I was in a shell. The illness broke it open and a new life began." His cross was a teacher.

The cross is also a means of salvation. Paul says, "In my flesh I am filling up what is lacking in the afflictions of Christ on behalf of his body, which is the church . . ." (Col 1:24). The ordained priest, and indeed every one of us who is a member of the general priesthood of all the baptized, has his or her own measure of pain to join with the sacrifice and surrender of Christ, the "high priest" (Heb 2:17) for the salvation and sanctification of the Church and the world. When the difficulties, contradictions, temptations, pains, and sorrows come — none of them need be wasted. All of them can be embraced as precious opportunities to join in the great work of redemption. When I hear confessions, give spiritual direction and visit the sick, I'm struck by the unsung heroism of many who fill up in their flesh "what is lacking in the afflictions of Christ on behalf of His body, which is the Church." God only knows the tremendous good they do for all of us in the Church and in the world!

In this connection I think of the courageous and joyful little Louisiana girl, Charlene Richard, who died of leukemia at the age of twelve. When the hospital chaplain visited her in her last days of illness she would regularly ask, "Who can I suffer for today?"

Thank God for the Catholic Church's biblical teaching about redemptive suffering (popularly expressed in the injunction "offer it up!") and for the traditional practice of "the morning offering" of all that each day entails.

I think of something I once heard a priest from Medjugorje say in regard to marriage. It was both humorous and profound. He said that whenever he marries a couple (according to a custom in his country) they bring with them a crucifix which they have selected. During the ceremony, as they join hands with one another, they also join hands with the crucifix. He tells them to take that crucifix home with them and put it in a prominent place. "Remember that from now on your husband will be your cross! Your wife will be your cross! Accept that cross. Love that cross. Live the daily dying to self that is involved in married love, the forgetting of self in thinking of the other. In that 'way of the cross' is your way to new life, to holiness, to salvation."

Each walk of life involves its particular cross or crosses and its own challenge and opportunities to sacrifice self for others. Just one example of that for the Catholic priest, religious brother and sister and some laypersons is the voluntary commitment to lifelong celibacy. It's made by many of us in the fervor and enthusiasm of young manhood or womanhood but living it out each day takes discipline and self-denial. When the temptations come, I sometimes think of those who struggle to keep their marriage vows or live a chaste, single life and I offer my small sacrifice and the surrender of myself to the Father on behalf of them, as well as for myself.

When the Church holds up for our edification and imitation the saints and particularly the martyrs, it's to encourage us to embrace the difficult things that life brings and that membership in the Church entails — not in a masochistic spirit but in the spirit of the Savior of the world for our good and the good of the whole world.

Not every cross, however, is the cross of Our Lord Jesus Christ. There are many crosses which we bring on ourselves that are not God's will for us. An example is the cross of resentment, bitterness, *lack of forgiveness.* This is a heavy cross which many carry against the will of the Lord. Forgiveness, beginning with the willingness to forgive and to start praying for the persons who hurt us is the call from the Lord. *Loneliness* is another cross that may be self imposed. Everyone has some experience of loneliness; but there is also a loneliness that comes from cutting ourselves off from humble and honest communion with God or with others, and from the unwillingness to reach out beyond ourselves to help and befriend our neighbors. One Sunday morning some years ago, when I made a regular telephone call to my very elderly mother (now 96) she told me that she was feeling down and lonely. I talked with her and said I'd call her back later in the day. When I did so, she was in a happy mood. I asked her why. She said that after we talked she decided to get dressed and go visit an elderly widow (a year older than herself) in an apartment several stories above her own. She probably tried to cheer up her friend, and in the process her own sadness and loneliness were lifted!

Many illnesses that can be offered sacrificially are still to be either prevented or abated by avoiding excess in the three "s's": sitting, stuffing and smoking! Care for our health, including proper exercise and diet, is the will of God for us. *Addictions* are also crosses but it is His will that we humble ourselves and seek the necessary help available to deal with them.

Besides self-made "ungodly" crosses, however, there is the genuine call to share in His cross — as an instrument of purification, teaching, and salvation. In fact, the fullness of the doctrine and moral guidance of the Church, which we're called to embrace and incorporate into our lives, makes no sense except in the light of the cross of Our Lord Jesus Christ. Living a life as a member of the community of the Church, participating in the give and take of involvement in that community, putting up with the unpleasant as well as the pleasant, abiding by Church discipline, and being obedient to her legitimate authority — all of this involves self-emptying; it involves the cross. Accepting the reality that the Church's members are human and sinful and that her leaders are of the same stock as the rest of us; experiencing and hopefully forgiving the hurts that inevitably come about in the Church, as in any family—even being tolerant of the dullness and irrelevance of many of our homilies! — involve the cross.

Following Christ and His Church's moral teachings and challenge in business and medicine, in politics and education, in single, married and family life means to embrace the cross. Accepting ourselves as we are - with our daily lives, our joys and sorrows, gifts and limitations, our responsibilities and vocations — is to accept the cross. Standing up for truth and human life and dignity when it's unpopular to do so and you're swimming against the current of the world, that's an experience of the cross. Allowing your own plans, ambitions and organizations to be shattered, when necessary, so that His mysterious plan can be accomplished, His kingdom come and His Church succeed — is to live the cross. To forget yourself and reach out in love and service and evangelization to others; to accept voluntarily self-denial and self-sacrifice for the sake of the kingdom (when all the ads say get all the satisfaction you can!) — is to follow the way of the cross.

"Enter through the narrow gate; for the gate is wide and the road broad that leads to destruction, and those who enter through it are many. How narrow the gate and constricted the road that leads to life. And those who find it are few" (Mt 7:13-14). The way of the cross is a ridiculous way in secular eyes. It's our living of His paschal mystery, dying and rising, dying to self, so we can truly and selflessly live (Jn 12:24-26). In the eyes of God, it's the way of Christ and the way of His Church — and it's *"the road that leads to life"*, *now and forever*!

OUR MISSION

G od sent His Son as a light-because of the darkness of the world. That "light shines in the darkness, and the darkness has not overcome it." (Jn 1:5). The Son sent His Church as "the light of the world ... A city set on a mountain ... a lamp ... (that) gives light to all in the house." (Mt 5:14-15).

That light is "the light of the human race" (Jn 1:3). Without it we don't know how to live, where we're going and how to get there. It's the light that lights up the meaning of human existence and the goal of all living. Smothering or ignoring it, we're in the darkness still.

If that light was ever needed in our world, it's needed today—when darkness has fallen on many even within the Church—when light and darkness, right and wrong, truth and error often become all mixed up and turned around.

To give an example, I've just finished reading an article about men and women of homosexual orientation. It appeared in a Catholic magazine I picked up from the vestibule of a church where I helped out this morning with Sunday Masses. An interview with a nun who works with Catholic gays and lesbians, the article has a lot of great and wonderful, sensitive and sensible things to say. I found it both enlightening and helpful, but also found it erroneous and harmful. My emotions in reading it included empathy, anger, sadness, joy, discouragement, feelings of being "out of it," pride about the Church — and a new determination to proclaim what that Church teaches.

The person interviewed believes the Church is wrong in not permitting long-term gay and lesbian sexual relationships. She questions whether Scripture actually condemns this. That Scripture does condemn homosexual acts is clear enough. The inspired authors of Scripture apparently didn't even imagine that we would come to the point where the people of God would be condoning long-term unisexual relationships as an alternative marital union.

She refers to the AIDS crisis as a call for greater empathy and understanding regarding the whole issue of homosexuality. God knows tremendous compassion is needed in this, as well many other areas of the human condition and struggle! How long will it take us to realize, however, that the AIDS crisis is crying out to a whole world: "Get back to the Creator's plan for sex and marriage!"

I mention this only as one example of what's happening in so many quarters of the Church today — especially in our country and parts of Europe. We're still singing "Onward Christian Soldiers" and shooting ourselves in the foot! On one level we're building the kingdom of God and on another we're undermining it.

There are many more issues beyond the sexual ones (though there is particular confusion in that area, with far reaching consequences). Every area of life including business, politics, science and technology, entertainment and the arts, medicine, social service and international relations, needs the moral guidance and light of Jesus and His

Church. But are we courageously proclaiming and following that "light of the human race?"

How many institutions and training programs for lay or clerical leaders, catechists or religious education coordinators have become tainted with false teachings! We're requiring our religion teachers and leaders to take courses from which they sometimes emerge having lost something of true religion!

We're sending our youth, often at great expense and sacrifice, to some colleges and universities in different parts of our country that bear the name Catholic but are no longer truly commited to the Lordship of Jesus Christ and the fullness of Catholic teaching. We're encouraging people to read "Catholic" literature which at times weakens rather than reinforces their faith and committment to the Church.

I'm pretty sure that the pastor (who was away) and most leaders of the parish where this magazine was set out disagree with the position of the nun in the article, and yet it's set out, probably without thought or notice, for parishioners to pick up. Actually (unaware of the magazine), I had said something in the homily of that same Sunday's Mass that was the exact opposite of what the article was promoting.

For a very long time now, especially since the Second Vatican Council, the attitude of many has been: If we can just find out the things that need to change in the teachings and practices of the Church, we'll bring the world back to God! Has it occurred to them (to us) that it may not be the teachings of the Church that have to change but the hearts and minds and lives of us all? *Why is change always "out there somewhere" and not right here within our very selves?* The fact is that a tremendous number of people have left the Church or been scandalized, confused, discouraged or disgruntled precisely because of changes — especially when they experience what they perceive as changes in long-standing moral or doctrinal teachings.

Is it merely coincidental that dioceses in our country that have experienced greater interest in the priesthood and more applicants for their seminaries are usually noted for little tolerance of moral, pastoral or liturgical deviations? Is it not significant that in those parts of the world, like Poland and Vietnam, where people have had to suffer for their faith, priestly and religious vocations have flourished?

Something similar is true of certain religious communities, like that of Mother Teresa of Calcutta, which offer a real challenge to their members and have been characterized by faithfulness to the Church, the Pope and to the authentic spirit and concept of religious life of their founders. People apparently are hunting for challenge and for the house Jesus talked about with "the foundation on rock" that will stand firm amidst the storms of controversy, the shifting sands of doubt, and all the winds of change(Lk 6:48). Whether they know it or not, they're hunting for the ancient and ever-new Church founded on the rock of St. Peter and all that Church is meant to be and proclaim.

In the cry for changes in the Church, the big distinction that many fail to make is between what can and should change and what can't and shouldn't. Changing the laws about Friday abstinence or even mandatory priestly celibacy is very different from changing laws about homosexual practices, birth control or teachings on heaven, hell and purgatory. Every law that is strictly a Church law, made by the Church, can be changed by the Church. When it's a question, however, of laws or teachings which the Church understands to be God's laws or teachings, the Church does not have the authority to change them. That's the case with such things as homosexual practices, birth control or the permanency of marriage. That's also the case with teachings like heaven, hell, purgatory and the Holy Eucharist.

Long ago Pope Paul VI warned about the influence of the Evil One in the affairs of the Church. He talked about "the smoke of Satan" even in the sanctuary. Is it any accident that many who undermine the teachings of the Church begin with or emphasize the denial of Satan himself, portraying those who believe in him as strictly "out of it". With that denial, often goes a denial of angels and the denial of hell.

Of course, Satan rejoices in all of this. It's exactly what he wants. He's an "undercover agent". Jesus calls him the great liar and deceiver, "a liar and the father of lies" (Jn 8:44). Deny him, forget him, ignore him — and he can go about his business unhampered and unnoticed — and in many quarters, that's exactly what he's doing!

The battle we're in is much more than what meets the eye and those who fight it better know what they're up against. It's not going to be won by mere human cleverness or arguments, power or programs but only by the power of God. "Finally, draw your strength from the Lord and from His mighty power. Put on the armor of God so that you may be able to stand firm against the tactics of the devil. For our struggle is not with flesh and blood but with the principalities, with the powers, with the world rulers of this present darkness, with the evil spirits in the heavens. Therefore, put on the armor of God, that you may be able to resist on the evil day and, having done everything, to hold your ground" (Eph 6:10-13).

We need to remember the words of Jesus when He first sent His disciples out to do His work. "Be shrewd as serpents and simple as doves" (Mt 10:16).

"Be shrewd as serpents": Have the wisdom, the discernment to spot evil and error, even when it comes "in sheep's clothing". Don't be taken in by it and do what you reasonably can to correct it — especially for the sake of others who may thereby be led astray.

Many of us have become overly tolerant of moral or doctrinal error even within the "family of the faith" (Gal 6:10). We're unaware that "all the (moral) evils in the world are ultimately traceable to error." 1 The apostles and early Fathers of the Church were so dedicated to the truth and pure doctrine that they regarded the opposite to be one of the worst of evils and one of the greatest violations of love of neighbor. They were ready to die for the divine truths that had been entrusted or handed down to them. It was on his way to imprisonment and martyrdom, that Paul pleads with the priests of his day, "Keep watch over yourselves and over the whole flock of which the holy Spirit has appointed you overseers, in which you tend the Church of God that he acquired with his own blood. I know that after my departure savage wolves will come among you, and they will not spare the flock. And from your own group, men will come forward perverting the truth to draw the disciples away after them. So be vigilant and remember that for three years, night and day, I unceasingly admonished each of you with tears" (Acts 20:28-31). To feed the flock rightly was the great commission Jesus gave to Peter and his successors and to the whole Church (Jn 21:15-17). If we wouldn't tolerate someone laying out poisoned or tainted food on the family table — how much more outraged should we be about the food that can help corrupt the mind and heart and lead to eternal death!

What to do in a particular situation when confronted with the propagation of error requires good judgment, genuine charity, respect for persons (especially superiors) and the guidance of the Holy Spirit.

Jesus says: "If your brother sins [against you], go and tell him his fault between you and him alone. If he listens to you, you have won over your brother. If he does not listen, take one or two others along with you, so that 'every fact may be established on the testimony of two or three witnesses.' If he refuses to listen to them, tell the church. If he refuses to listen even to the church, then treat him as you would a Gentile or a tax collector" (Mt 18:15-17). Talk to the individual who is propagating error and when that is unsuccessful, "take one or two others along with you" (when feasible) and if still unsuccessful, contact the person's superior. When others are being misled and you're confident about the true teaching, it may be called for that you correct an error right on the spot — especially when no other opportunity will be available. (I'm not normally recommending this during someone else's Sunday morning homily!) This should always be done in the spirit of the Lord, relying on Him, and not just "grinding an ax."

Also *be simple as doves.* Don't be blind to all the genuine good that's going on. Goodness, new life, truth and "unity which has the Spirit as its origin" (Ep 4:3) — are all gifts of God. Wherever you find them, thank God for them, affirm them, encourage them, and pray that they continue to grow. "Do not be conquered by evil but conquer evil with good" (Rom 12:21). What's true in the family and community at home is true in the family and community of the Church. Just to criticize can pull down. To affirm is to build up. Most people can grow only in an atmosphere of affirmation.

We need to recognize the good in the Church and the many who are working for the good in order to keep our balance and stay sane and hopeful. We need also to see that many who sow seeds of doubt and confusion and false teaching are personally blinded to the evil of what they are doing and think they are crusaders for truth and justice. We are called to love them while hating what they do.

Above all, however, we need to remember that it's *His* Church and He'll never abandon it. We have to keep asking and praying and working and offering ourselves and our sacrifices for the Church — in our flesh "filling up what is lacking in the afflictions of Christ on behalf of his body which is the Church" (Col 1:24). We are called to do all this in peace and in confidence in Him who will accept it and use it for good.

The story is told that Pope John XXIII would sometimes, at night, look out of his window over the city of Rome and say : "Well, Lord, it's your Church — and I'm going to bed!"

In 1961 Pope John XXIII wrote his famous social encyclical "Mater and Magistra" referring to the Church as "Mother and Teacher". The reaction to that title on the part of some was "Mater si — Magistra no!"

Today, I believe there are *many sons and daughters of the Church who would also no longer recognize the Church as their Mater or Mother*. The title is seldom, if ever, used anymore — yet it remains beautiful and meaningful. St. Cyprian, bishop of Carthage, a father of the Church, wrote in 251 A.D.: "He cannot have God for his Father who does not have the Church for his Mother." [2]

How much have we received from that Mother! From her knee so many of us received the heritage of the true faith, the cleansing waters of baptism and the repeated gift of reconciliation, the Bread of Life for our journey, the companionship of Mary and all the saints, the fellowship of believers and so much more. So, don't bite the hand that feeds you! When you do: "Hey, you're talking about my Mamma!"

The Church is also Magistra. She is the teacher of the nations — the light of the world. The thing that was characteristic of Jesus was that "he taught them as one having authority, and not as their scribes" (Mt 7:29). We should expect His Church to do the same! Jesus didn't say "I think this is the way it is" or "This is my opinion". He said "Amen, amen I say to you!" [3] The great Protestant Scripture scholar Joachim Jeremias says that together with the use of the word "Abba" (Father, Daddy, Papa), the thing that was especially distinct about Jesus Christ was this regular use of "Amen, Amen". It was a decidedly authoritative way of speaking, unique to Jesus Christ. [4] He taught like no person had taught before Him. His words were definite, final and infallible. The authority of Jesus has been passed on to His Church. "All power in heaven and on earth has been given to me. Go therefore, and make disciples of all nations... teaching them...And behold, I am with you always, until the end of the age" (Mt 28:18-20). It's not the Church's authority on her own. It's the authority of Jesus who speaks through His Church! How much that clear authoritative voice is needed in the world today!

The Book of Ecclesiastes says "Nothing is new under the sun" (Eccl 1:9b). That's certainly true of almost all Christian heresies. Those we run up against today have usually, in one form or the other, been around before. Today, however, it's not just two or three doctrines that are under attack. Almost every teaching of the Catholic Church has been opened up to question by one "Catholic" theologian or the other.

Some even seem to think that Pope John XXIII, in calling together the Second Vatican Council, intended to encourage all this. Nothing could be further from the truth! John XXIII (as one could tell from his own personal <u>Journal Of A Soul</u> and in many other ways) was a very orthodox and faithful son of the Church. In Pope John's opening speech to the Council, Oct. 11, 1962 in St. Peter's Basilica he said: "***The greatest concern of the Ecumenical Council is this: that the sacred deposit of Christian doctrine should be guarded and taught more efficaciously.***" He added, "It is necessary first of all that the Church should never depart from the sacred patrimony of truth received from the Fathers." He did make it clear, however, that "The substance of the ancient doctrine of the deposit of faith is one thing, and the way in which it is presented is another."[5]

Pope John has been responsibly quoted as saying that the greatest heresy of his time was a **new Pelagianism**, modeled after that of Pelagius of old. The new Pelagianism believes in human effort alone and ignores or downplays the supernatural — the work of grace and the power of God.

Theologian, Karl Rahner, long ago penned an article (too seldom quoted) in which he stated what he considered to be a great modern day all-pervasive heresy. For him, it was **the failure to emphasize the love of God over the love of neighbor**. He pointed out that unless we make God's love and God's will primary — we no longer know what is truly good for our neighbor and what it means to sincerely love God's children. The door is open to every kind of aberration under the heading of "compassion" or "love"! A prime example of this is so-called "mercy killing"!

Fr. John Hardon S.J., author and for many years professor of comparative religions, talks about a *new paganism* that has engulfed the world, especially the Western world and infected many in the Church. Different from the paganism of old, the new paganism, he says, is "monotheistic." There is only one god and his name in English is always capitalized: **I**. The individual, the self has been exalted beyond anything the world has ever known before. Each person becomes the final judge and jury about right and wrong and even about the mysteries of faith." Truth is what **I** think is true . . . good is what **I** choose as good for me." [6]

Whether it's to counteract the new Pelagianism, new paganism or new "compassion" and "love" — how much we need the clarity of the teaching Church in our world today!

How much also do we need ongoing genuine spiritual renewal and spiritual direction—grounded in the truth. Much that passes today for spiritual renewal and direction has lost its moorings. What ever happened to Ignatius of Loyola's "Rules For Thinking with the Church"? For him this was an essential part of the Spiritual Exercises. Divorced from the teaching Church, spiritual renewal and direction can either be destructive or at least misleading. What true renewal can there be that is not rooted in truth? What other sure guide have we been given for religious truth than Him who is "the truth" (Jn 14:16) and the Church He established as "the pillar and foundation of truth" (1 Tim 3:15)? What is the value of any spiritual director who does not himself or herself take direction from the Church of Jesus and the earthly shepherd of all shepherds, the Pope?

That a great blindness and deception has engulfed the earth and many in the Church is not however a cause for despair or even discouragement. Could it not be that God who can bring light out of darkness and good out of evil has permitted this in order to wake us up to how far astray we can go without Him and His Church to guide us and how greatly we need His light, His grace and His Church? Alongside the deluge of evil in the world and in the Church, there is available an ocean of grace. "Where sin abounded, grace did more abound" (Rom 5:20 Challoner-Rheims Ed). It is the hope of John Paul II who knows the condition of the world better than anyone that the 21st century will be the brightest and greatest of all Christian eras. But this depends on you and me. Every day, one and all, he reminds us, we need to be converted anew. The salvation of the world depends on each of us — our own personal holiness, which mysteriously affects everyone else. It depends also on my prayers and sacrifices, my ever-growing openness to Jesus, His Spirit and His Church, my witness of life and my efforts to share with others all that I have received. More than ever before we need to know our Catholic faith, live our faith and be ready to die for our faith. It is the time right now for what John Paul II calls "a new evangelization." It is time to hear the call he issued to the bishops of the United States for a reevangelization of our land. One instrument of this is the new universal catechism of the Catholic Church. Let's welcome it, digest it, live it and share its contents with others. [7]

Those who don't want the Church as teacher, have already set the stage for ignoring, rejecting, discrediting or giving biased interpretations of the catechism coming out of Rome. This catechism, however, the first of its kind in 400 years, can be a tremendous means of helping to restore unity of faith and of bringing the light of Christ to bear on the hearts and minds of many who walk in darkness and confusion.

Hopefully, there will be such a reaction to the darkness and confusion that people throughout the world will rejoice in the light of the new catechism and begin again to welcome *the gift of the Church* — as foreshadowed long ago in the words of the prophets about the temple and the Jerusalem of old:

"In days to come, the mountain of the Lord's house shall be established as the highest mountain and raised above the hills. All nations shall stream toward it; many peoples shall come and say: 'Come, let us climb the Lord's mountain, to the house of the God of Jacob, that he may instruct us in his ways, and we may walk in his paths!' For from Zion shall go forth instruction, and the word of the Lord from Jerusalem" (Is 2:2-3; Mi 4:1-2).

To see this prophesy fulfilled in the years ahead — that "many people shall come and say: 'Come, let us climb the Lord's mountain, to the house of the God of Jacob, that he may instruct us in his ways, and we may walk in his paths!'" — for this let us work and pray, entrusting it all to her who is the Mother of Jesus the Light, and model and mother of the New Jerusalem, the Church of God. Mary, our Queen and Mother, pray for us!

APPENDIX

Why do you say that the contraceptive pill could cause abortions?

The sixth edition of <u>Danforth's Obstetrics and Gynecology</u> textbook, 1990, says, "The production of glycogen by the endometrial glands is diminished by the ingestion of oral contraceptives, which ***impairs the survival of the blastocyst in the uterine cavity.***" [1] In other words all oral contraceptives hinder or endanger the survival in the womb of the newly fertilized egg, the new human being. They all alter the uterine lining in such a way that it is hostile to implantation of the one week-old-embryo.

There are two categories of pills. One (rarely used today) contains progestin only; it is sometimes called the "mini-pill". The other is the "combined pill" containing estrogen and progestin.

Actually there are three mechanisms through which the pill accomplishes its birth control effect. 1) It attempts to suppress ovulation. 2) It thickens the cervical mucus in such a way that it becomes more difficult for the sperm to reach the egg. 3) It alters the lining of the uterus so that implantation is impaired. The progestin-only pill; Norplant® (a progestin-only implant); and the IUD rely heavily on this third mechanism — altering the uterine lining — to accomplish their purpose. The combined pill relies mostly on the two other effects. With the combined pill, ovulation is impaired and a mucus blockage is formed against the passage of the sperm. These first two effects, however, do not always work. Break-through ovulation sometimes occurs (more often with the low dose pills used today), and the mucus does not always obstruct the male seed. Fertilization of the egg does at times take place. The third effect, when conception occurs, is the probable rejection of the fertilized egg — a human life and human being. It is true that sometimes the new life does survive, and women become pregnant and bear children even though they are on the pill. The womb, however, has been so altered by the pill that this is unlikely; it is not properly prepared to sustain human life. In fact, it is prepared to reject or not receive a fertilized egg.

The standard *Physicians' Desk Reference* (PDR), which all doctors use, states in the 1994 edition, "Combination oral contraceptives act by suppression of gonadotrophins. Although the primary mechanism of this action is inhibition of ovulation, other alterations include *changes* in the cervical mucus (which increase the difficulty of sperm entry into the uterus) and *the endometrium (which reduce the likelihood of implantation)." (Words in parenthesis are also from* PDR*)*. 2

Dr. J.C. Willke, a general practitioner with a specialty in gynecology and the guiding spirit of the National Right to Life Committee, is one of the most knowledgeable persons in our country on the abortion issue. Dr. Willke makes it clear that contraception is not part of NRLC's agenda; but in the 1991 revised edition of his book Abortion (considered by some "the Bible" on the subject and edited with his wife, Barbara, a nurse), they repeat unchanged what they had originally written in 1981. Referring to the lower estrogen content of the pills commonly used today, they state: "The earlier high-estrogen pills largely prevented ovulation. The newer low-estrogen pills allow 'breakthrough' ovulation in up to 20% or more of the months used. Such a released ovum is fertilized perhaps 10% of the time. These tiny new lives which result, at our present 'guesstimations', in 1% or 2% of the pill months, do not survive. The reason is that *at one week of life, this tiny new boy or girl cannot implant in the womb lining and dies. These are micro-abortions.*" [3]

What about the IUD?

As described by Dr. Willke, "The intrauterine device, commonly referred to as an IUD, or a coil (in Europe), is a small plastic or metal device that is inserted into the cavity of the uterus through the vagina." [4]

The U.S. Food and Drug Administration years ago in a 1978 official report on the various types of IUDs summarized its findings by stating that they all "interfere in some manner with the implantation of the fertilized ovum in the uterine cavity." [5]

More recently, however, there have been attempts to say that a high percentage of the action of the IUD is to prevent fertilization. Such a claim has yet to be scientifically established. A 1990 report on contraception delivered at the Congress of the World Federation of Doctors who Respect Human Life states, *"The IUD is primarily an early abortive device.* Implantation of the embryo is prevented by a reactive inflammation of the endometrium. Even the copper content of the modern IUD makes no difference to this principle. Likewise, a more recent statement regarding the purely protective effect of the IUD is unconvincing." [6]

What about Norplant® — the under-the-skin implant and the recently approved Depo-Provera® (every three months) injection for contraception?

Like the "mini-pill", both of these drugs are progestin-only. They rely on altering the uterine lining as one of the ways to accomplish their purpose and have possible harmful side effects.

Dr. Thomas Hilgers, Director of the Pope Paul VI Institute for Reproductive Study, exposed some of Norplant's hurtful effects (so much now in the news) in a paper presented in February of '92. He explained that with the five year implant, break-through ovulation can take place on an average of almost 50% of the cycles, after the first year. Thus fertilization can frequently occur with the uterine wall not prepared for it. *This can result in micro-abortions*. "In nearly 90 percent of endometrial samples, the endometrium is disturbed. This mechanism of action renders Norplant an *abortifacient*. The exact incidence of its abortifacient properties is not yet known; however, it is clear that this mechanism exists and undoubtedly occurs." [7]

Depo-Provera® has been used for endometrial or renal cancer but has only more recently been approved as a contraceptive. It's action, as described in the <u>Physicians Desk Reference</u>, ". . . inhibits the secretion of gonadotropins which, in turn, prevents follicular maturation and ovulation and **results in endometrial thinning**. These actions produce its contraceptive effect." "Endometrial thinning"—rendering the uterus inhospitable to implantation—could cause early abortions. The <u>PDR</u> lists many possible side effects from the drug.[8]

If all of this is true (about the abortive potential of the pill, IUD, Norplant and contraceptive injection) why don't we hear more about it?

We're treading on an area that is deeply entrenched in the practice of couples, pharmaceutical companies and most Ob-Gyn specialists. Profit and a way of life are at stake. Drug companies and the majority of gynecological professionals **don't want people to know**. It's easy to prescribe pills etc. It takes time to teach **Natural Family Planning**. There is also no personal financial gain in **NFP** - but it **would save patients untold expenses.** Sad to say there may even be Ob-Gyn doctors who are not completely aware of the abortive potential of these drugs and devices because of relying on the drug companies or the medical schools for such information by whom it is often not highlighted. Certainly there are many priests, religious and some seminary professors who are not sufficiently well informed in this regard.

Organizations and individuals who are helping to make people aware of such facts are the following:
- Dr. and Mrs. J.C. Willke in their book <u>Abortion</u>
- Dr. Thomas Hilgers, Director of the Pope Paul VI Institute for Reproductive Study
- The John XXIII Center for medical-moral research and education
- The Couple to Couple League for Natural Family Planning
- The Family of the Americas Organization for NFP
- The American Life League
- Human Life International
- World Federation of Doctors who Respect Human Life
- Pharmacists for Life

Why doesn't my doctor say this?

This seems to be a blind spot with many otherwise good doctors — for reasons already mentioned. Thank God, however, for those courageous Ob-Gyn physicians in different parts of the country (I've personally become aware of about 27) and family specialists who have abandoned or never taken up the use of contraceptives in their practice. They will not hide the abortive potential of the pill, IUD, etc.

What about RU 486 and the contraceptive vaccine?

The RU 486, developed in France, is a *directly* abortive drug, with some other possible uses. As a abortifacient, it is taken after pregnancy. Dr. Willke states clearly: "**It kills a developing unborn baby after her heart has begun to beat.**"[9]

The so-called contraceptive vaccine is also abortive. Even the newspaper reports on it admitted that it has its effect mainly by interfering with the implantation of the fertilized ovum.

The report at the Congress of the World Federation of Doctors Who Respect Human Life states: "...RU-486 (progesterone antagonist) and Epostane (progesterone synthesis blocker) combined with prostaglandins,. . .enable medicinal abortion up to the later stages of pregnancy, thus replacing most of the surgical abortions, which are burdensome in many ways. There is also the 'anti-baby' vaccine (anti-HCG-vaccine) soon to come into use, which is also a method of early abortion." The report goes on to say, "Thus the perfected killing of unborn life takes its place in our society, resulting in a veritable holocaust. Thus it could be said that the great tragedy of the turn of the century is the loss of human lives which should be able to seek their own destinies and are prevented from doing so." [10]

Besides its abortive effect, Dr. and Mrs. Willke in their book Abortion show why RU 486 "will cause the death of thousands of women in Third World countries" and great harm also to children who are not aborted. "This powerful, poisonous, artificial steroid will kill most of these unborn babies, but not all." "It will cause severe fetal deformity in surviving babies..." [11]

But isn't it difficult to use Natural Family Planning?

Restraint is required in the use of every pleasure God has given us: food, drink, sight, sound, sex, etc. There are many times in every marriage that circumstances, such as illness or unavoidable separation, call for restraint. Restraint and sacrifice for the sake of the kingdom of God are necessities and bring a blessing. "Whoever wishes to come after me must deny himself, take up his cross and follow me" (Mt 16:24).

Actually the days of abstinence each month are usually less than ten. It has been the experience of NFP teachers that couples preparing for marriage see the restraint aspect as the main obstacle in accepting this natural method when they are learning about it; but afterwards, in marriage, once they have begun to use Natural Family Planning, they often see it as a positive gift. The very limiting of their sexual relationship causes them to appreciate it all the more; what you can have at any time can lose some of its attractiveness. NFP couples speak about a repeated experience of courtship and honeymoon over and over in their marriage. They also are challenged to find, during the fertile times, other non-genital ways of expressing their affection; and this enhances their relationship and love.

Is Natural Family Planning really that effective?

A Sept. 18th,1993 article on Natural Family Planning in the British Medical Journal (Vol.307) by Dr. R.E.J. Ryder reviews a number of NFP effectiveness studies from various parts of the world. He states: "increasingly studies show that rates equivalent to those with other contraceptive methods are readily achieved (thru NFP) in the developed and developing worlds. **Indeed, a study of 19,843 poor women in India had a pregnancy rate approaching zero.** Natural family planning is cheap, effective, without side effects, and may be particularly acceptable to and efficacious among people in areas of poverty." (Emphasis added)

A government study of couples using the Sympto-Thermal Method, conducted between 1976 and 1978 by the US Department of Health, Education, and Welfare, actually showed a 100% effectiveness among couples who used the method correctly. Since such a high effectiveness rate cannot be sustained in a large population, promoters of the Sympto-Thermal Method modestly (!) claim 99% effectiveness. [12]

But it doesn't seem to work for me!

Maybe you're not using the method correctly. Though it is possible to learn a method through reading, personal instruction or classes seem to produce much better results.

Contact with the instructor afterwards, while the method is being used, can also be helpful. If, however, you find one particular method confusing, try another.

The two most commonly used methods of Natural Family Planning are the Billings Ovulation Method and the Sympto-Thermal Method. The Ovulation Method is based on the external observation of the cervical mucus discharge. The Sympto-Thermal Method combines this also with observing the body's daily waking temperature, taken with a basal-body thermometer. Physical changes in the cervix can be another indicator of fertile days. Besides these three basic signs some women have also noticed additional and secondary signs of fertility.

Though some have found that improved nutrition can be a great help in regulating the menstrual cycle, modern day NFP, different from rhythm, does not depend upon a regular cycle. In fact it can be used by every woman regardless of cycle irregularities such as those associated with coming off the pill or Depo-provera, post-partum, peri-menopause etc. At headquarters of the various NFP organizations there is a constant effort to perfect and simplify the method. When you need expert advice, contact the experts in the field.

What about poor people and the uneducated and Third World countries?

Natural Family Planning is taught around the world, including the Third World, with amazing success. The Sisters of Charity, under the guidance of Mother Teresa of Calcutta, teach it to the poorest of the poor. The Family of the Americas' (an NFP organization) has brought it to Red

China with enthusiastic reception by ordinary people and great cooperation from members of the country's government and medical profession.

Uneducated people who are close to nature are often more in touch with the God-made cycles of fertility and the natural signs of it than many of the educated. Using artificial contraceptives can be costly and even more so with the adverse side effects that often follow. NFP costs little or nothing to learn and to use.

It need also be noted that in our country there is great conciousness about ecology and health, diets and health foods, and much publicity about the ill effects of such things as tobacco, drugs and alcohol. How much more reason, therefore, to promote a *natural* method of family planning that requires no drugs or devices and has no harmful side effects.

What about overpopulation? Don't we have to drastically reduce the number of people on the earth?

Several books have exposed the fallacies behind the overpopulation myth. In particular I would mention those by Jacqueline Kasun, [13] Robert Sassone [14] and several by Julian Simon, professor of Business Administration at the University of Maryland. [15] Simon states that: *"In the 1980s a revolution occurred in scientific views about the effect of population growth on economic development: economists stopped asserting that population increases must exhaust natural resources and preclude economic growth."*[16]

Actually the population myths are varied; they have to

do with food, space, the environment, economic growth etc. A well-documented report from Human Life International deals with eight basic fallacies or myths and authoritatively refutes each one. [17] We cannot cover all this here but just touch on two of the most common fallacies, relating to food and space.

Gandhi of India used to say, "There is enough in the world to take care of our needs but not our greeds!" It is certainly God's will that we share our bread with one another, as well as our technical skills and equipment. Colin Clark, formerly director of the Agricultural Economic Institute at Oxford University estimated, in 1972, that *the earth could raise enough food for an American style diet for roughly 35 billion people (approximately seven times the number that live on the earth) while leaving nearly half of the land surface in conservation areas*! [18] American farmers alone (an extremely small portion of our work force) have so much surplus that they must export much of their crop or the prices will drop so low that the farms will go out of business. The U.S. government even pays farmers at times not to plant! [19]

The problems of starvation in Africa are due mainly to their own government policies and civil wars, rather than lack of food or overpopulation. Africa is one of the world's least densely populated continents and the famines of the 70s and 80s occurred in sparsely populated countries. [20] All of this is true of Somalia, Ethiopia and Rwanda as well.

Another myth is that planet earth is too small. Anyone who has traveled extensively and seen so many unpopulated areas of our country and elsewhere has reason to wonder about any legitimate foundation for this statement. Jacqueline Kasun, Professor of Economics at Humboldt

State University, *includes in one of her publications the fact that all the people in the world could be housed in the state of Texas, giving each one enough square feet of space (about the size of the typical American home) and leaving the rest of the world empty*! [21] Actually a figure like this is arrived at by simple (!) mathematics: dividing the number of square feet taken up by the state of Texas by the number of people on the face of the earth. *Today, with 5.5 billion people, each person would still get 1330 square feet*!

The fact is that many nations are shrinking in population and dying out through birth control, abortion and sterilization. They are not reproducing themselves and maintaining their population levels. This is generally the case throughout the Western world, with few exceptions. Because of this, it has become necessary in many European countries to import guest workers to take jobs that otherwise would not be carried out. Several countries also have national programs to encourage couples to bear children. This is not only true in France and Germany but also in Japan and Malaysia. The small republic of Singapore has decided to do away with its birth control program. One official of Singapore's population planning unit responsible for the new policies warned that otherwise "the current population of 2.6 million will start shrinking precariously in 2010 and nosedive towards eventual extinction." [22] **Where can I get more information about Natural Family Planning and other related issues like those touched on in this Appendix?**

Family Life Offices of each Catholic Diocese.

The Couple to Couple League International
NFP Organization
Sympto-Thermal Method
Box 111184, Cincinnati, OH 45211
Phone: (513) 661-7612
John Kippley, Director

Family of the Americas
NFP Organization
Ovulation Method
Box 1170, Dunkirk, MD 20754
Phone: (800) 443-3395
Mercedes Wilson, Director

Other Sources Referred To:
Pope Paul VI Institute for Reproductive Study
6901 Mercy Rd.
Omaha, NE 68106
Phone: (402) 390-6600
Dr. Thomas Hilgers, Director

The Pope John XXIII Center
for Medical-Moral Research and Education
186 Forbes Rd., Braintree, MA 02184
Phone: (617) 848-6965
Rev. Russell E. Smith, S.T.D., Director

Other Sources: (continued)

Monthly Publication — "Ethics and Medics"
Senior Editor: Fr. Albert Moraczewski, O.P., Ph.D.
Phone: (314) 533-2679

Pharmacists for Life
Pro-Life Organization
Box 130, Ingomar, PA 1512
Phone: (800) 227-8359
Bogamir Kuhar, President

Priests for Life
Pro-Life Organization
Box 141172, Staten Island, NY 10314
Phone: (914) 937-8243
Fr. Frank Pavone, Nat. Director

World Federation of Doctors
Who Respect Human Life
c/o Dr. Phillipe Schepens
Serruysloan 76-3
B-8400 Ostend, Belgium
Phone: 59-80-08-60

Human Life International
Largest International Pro-Life
and Pro-Family Organization
7845 East Airpark Rd.,
Gaithersburg, MD 20879
Phone: (301) 670-7884
Fr. Paul Marx, Director

References and Endnotes

Chapter 1
[1] <u>Columbia Magazine</u>, (New Haven, CT, Dec. 1985), back cover.

Chapter 2
[1] Richard John Neuhaus, <u>The Catholic Moment</u>, (San Francisco: Harper & Row Publishers, 1987). (Emphasis added.)

[2] Michael Sheehan, "Seizing the Catholic Moment," <u>The Catholic Answer</u>, (Huntington, IN, Our Sunday Visitor, Inc., July-August 1989). (Emphasis added.)

[3] Walter M. Abbott, S.J., gen. ed., Vatican Council II, "Dogmatic Constitution on the Church", <u>Documents of Vatican II</u>, 13th ed. (America Press/Association Press, 1966), Art. 8, pp. 22-23. (Emphasis added).

Chapter 3
[1] Ibid. "Message to Humanity," issued at the beginning of the Second Vatican Council, by its Fathers, with the endorsement of the Supreme Pontiff [Oct. 20, 1962], p. 4.

Chapter 4
[1] Dietrich Bonhoffer, <u>Life Together</u> (New York: Harper & Row Publishers, 1954), p. 112. (Emphasis added.)

2   Earl Jabay, <u>Precisely How To Take Care of Yourself</u> (Plainsfield, NJ: Logos International, 1979), p. 67. (Emphasis added.)

3   "Apostolic Exhortation on Reconciliation and Penance", Dec. 11, 1984, reported in <u>Origins</u>, (Dec. 20, 1984 National Catholic News Service, 1312 Mass. Ave., N.W., Washington DC 20005), #18.

4   Cyril Auboyneanetal, <u>Words from Heaven: Messages of Our Lady from Medjugorje</u>, 2nd ed. (Birmingham, AL: St. James Publishing, 1990), p. 21. See also index under "Confession", p. 94.

Chapter 5

1   St. Augustine, a Father of the Church (354-430) wrote: "I would not believe the Gospel, if the authority of the Catholic Church did not move me." (C. epict. fund, 5.5: CSEL 25:197) quoted in <u>New Catholic Encyclopedia</u>, (New York, McGraw Hill Co., 1966), p. 387.

2   Vatican Council II, "Dogmatic Constitution on Divine Revelation", #8a, p.116.

3   "Letter to the Ephesians", <u>The Faith of the Early Fathers</u>, Vol.1, selected and translated by William H. Jurgens, (Collegeville, MN: The Liturgical Press), p.18 [7,2],#39

4   Collegeville, MN: The Liturgical Press, 1970, 3 vols.

5   Vatican Council II, "Dogmatic Constitution on Divine Revelation", #8b, p. 116.

[6] Martin Luther, letter to Albrecht, Duke of Brandenburg in Prussia, [1532], <u>Weimar Edition of Luther's Works in German</u>, translated by Helga Whittaker Interpreters Service, (Weimar, Germany: Hermann Bohlaus Publisher, 1910), vol. 30, p. 30.

[7] Sisters of the Visitation of Wilmington, Delaware, comp., <u>Life and characteristics of Rt. Rev. Alfred A. Curtis, D.D.,</u> [Feb. 14, 1872], (New York: P.J. Kennedy and Sons Publishers, 1913), pp. 31-32.

[8] "Letter to the Corinthians", (ca. A.D. 80), <u>The Faith of the Early Fathers</u>, vol. 1, p. 10, (42, 1), #20.

[9] "Adversus Haereses-Against Heresies", <u>The Faith of the Early Fathers</u>, p. 90, (3,3,3). #211

[10] Ibid. pp. 90-91, (3,4,1), #213. (Emphasis added.)

[11] Vatican Council II, "Declaration on Religious Freedom", # 14. (Emphasis added.)

[12] Ibid. "Pastoral Constitution on the Church in the Modern World", # 27.

[13] Ibid. # 51.

[14] Ibid. # 80.

Chapter 6
[1] "Letter to the Magnesians",: <u>The Faith of the Early Fathers</u>, vol. 1, p. 19 [6,1], #44.

[2] Ibid. "Letter to the Smyrnaeans", p. 25 [8,1], #65.

[3] Ibid. "Letter to the Philadelphians", p. 23 [7,1], #58a.

[4] The Faith of the Early Fathers, Vol. 1, p.220-221, [4], #555-556. (Emphasis added.)

Chapter 7

[1] Scott Hahn, Scripture professor, Franciscan University of Steubenville, OH (former Presbyterian pastor and seminary professor) on audio-cassette, Peter and the Papacy, St. Joseph Communications, Inc., Box 720 W. Covina, CA 91793.

[2] Ibid. Also Gerhard Maier (Protestant scholar) says that "Nowadays a broad concensus" of scholars hold this. "The Church in the Gospel of Matthew", Biblical Interpretation and the Church, (Nashville, TN: Thomas Nelson, Inc. Publishers, 1985, D.A. Carson, Editor) p. 58

[3] Grand Rapids, MI: Zondervan Publishing House, 1987, p. 303. (Emphasis added.)

[4] New American Bible, footnote on Matthew 16:19.

[5] Oscar Cullman, Peter (Philadelphia, PA: Westminister Press, 1962).

[6] The Faith of the Early Fathers, Vol. 1, pp. 6-13.

[7] Ibid. p. 90 [3,3,2]. #210. (Emphasis added.)

Chapter 8

[1] David Wilkerson, The Cross and the Switchblade (Old Tappan, NJ: Spire Books, Fleming H. Revell Co. Publishers, 1962).

[2] George Martin, An Introduction to the Catholic Charismatic Renewal (Ann Arbor, MI: Servant Publications rev. ed., 1986), p. 14.

[3] Pope John Paul II, address to the Council of the International Catholic Charismatic Renewal Office, "Charismatics: Faithful to the Church", [March 17, 1992,] The Pope Speaks (Huntington, IN: Our Sunday Visitor, July/Aug. '92), vol. 37, no. 4, p.239.

[4] Quoted in U.S. Bishops' Liaison Committee's "Pastoral Statement on the Catholic Charismatic Renewal" [March 1984], (Washington, DC, Publication #931, Office of Publishing and Promoting Services, USCC), p. 18

[5] Ibid. p. 19. (Emphasis added.)

[6] Kilian McDonnell & George T. Montague, Editors, "Christian Initiation and Baptism in the Holy Spirit: Evidence from the First Eight Centuries" synopsized in a booklet Fanning the Flame. (Collegeville, MN: Liturginal Press, 1991).

[7] The Pope Speaks, address to the Council of the International Catholic Charismatic Renewal Office, [March 17, 1992], vol. 37, no. 4, pp. 239-240.

[8] Ibid., p. 241.

[9] St. Augustine, In Ioannem Tract. 32,8: Pl 35, 1646, as quoted in The Documents of Vatican II, "Decree on Priestly Formation (Optatam Totius)", #9, p. 446.

[10] Prayer of Pope John XXIII to the Holy Spirit for the Success of the Ecumenical Council, The Documents of Vatican II, p. 793.

Chapter 9

[1] "Letter to Smyrnaeans", The Faith of the Early Fathers, Vol. 1, p. 25 [8,1] #65. See also New Catholic Encyclopedia (New York: McGraw Hill, 1967), vol. III, p. 261.

[2] Rudolf Ehman M.D., Dresden, Sept. 20-23, 1990 p. 2 (Emphasis added.)

Chapter 10

[1] Santa Barbara, CA: Queenship Publishing Co., 1993

[2] Vatican Council II, "Dogmatic Constitution on the Church", #51, p. 84.

Chapter 11

[1] "A Treatise Against the Heresy of Noetus", [Cap. 9-12: PG 10, 815-819] in The Liturgy of the Hours, 4 vols., (New York: Catholic Book Publishing Co., 1975), vol. 1, p. 371.

[2] "Letter to Smyrnaeans", The Faith of the Early Fathers, p. 25, [6,2], #64 (Emphasis added.)

3 "First Apology", [inter A.D. 148-155], <u>The Faith of the Early Fathers</u>, p. 55, [66]. #128 (Emphasis added.)

4 National Catholic Register Newspaper, (March 15, 1992), p. 1.

5 Vatican Council II, "Constitution on the Sacred Liturgy", # 10, p. 142.

6 <u>Lutherans and Catholics in Dialogue</u>, (Washington, DC: USCC, 1970), vol. 14, p. 193.

7 <u>The Unity We Seek</u>, (New York: Paulist Press, 1977), p. 39. (Emphasis added.)

8 Vatican Council II, "Constitution on the Sacred Liturgy," # 10, p. 142.

Chapter 12
1 <u>New Catholic Encyclopedia</u>, Vol. 8, p. 1118, 1967.

2 <u>Clarion Herald</u>, Jan. 30, 1992 (New Orleans, LA, Clarion Herald Publishing Co.), p.3

3 J.L.G. Balado, <u>The Story of Taize</u>, new rev. ed. (London: A.R. Mowbray & Co. Ltd., 1981), p. 46. (Emphasis added.)

4 Anglican-Roman Catholic International Commission, <u>The Final Report</u>, "Authority in the Church II" [Windsor 1981], 3rd ed. (Cincinnati, OH: Forward Movement Publications, N.W. Washington D.C.: Office of Publishing Services, USCC), Art. 9, p. 85. (Emphasis added.)

Chapter 13

Chapter 13

Chapter 13

GIFT OF THE CHURCH

5 Ibid., Art. 26, p. 93. (Emphasis added.)

Chapter 13

1 Scott Hahn, on audio cassette, <u>Protestant Minister Becomes Catholic</u>. Scott Hahn and his wife, Kimberly, have also produced a three audio cassette series dealing with the birth control issue; the series is called "Life Giving Love". All these and other talks by him on various Catholic teachings are available from St. Joseph Communications, Inc., Box 720, West Covina, CA 91793, Phone: (818) 331-3549.

2 John T. Noonan, Jr., <u>Contraception</u> (New York, NY, Mentor-Omega Books, The New American Library, 1965), p. 120. For a similar reference, see Augustine "Marriage and Concupiscence" where he speaks of "poisons of sterility", quoted in Noonan, p. 171. Also from John A. Hardon, S.J., <u>The Catholic Catechism</u> (Garden City, NY, Doubleday & Company, Inc., 1975), p. 367: "Given the widespread contraceptive practice of the first century of the Christian era, euphemistically referred to as 'using magic' and 'using drugs,' it is logical to see in the New Testament prohibition of *mageia* and *pharmakeia* an implicit condemnation of contraception. This is especially true when the contexts (Ga. 5:20 and Rev. 21:8,22:15) refer to sins against chastity. The *Didache*, which explicitly condemned abortion, also implicitly condemned contraception. The early Christians were told in four successive precepts: 'You shall not use magic. You shall not use drugs. You shall not procure abortion. You shall not destroy a new-born child.'

182

Records from the practices of those times tell us that the people would first try some magical rites or resort to sorcery to avoid conception. If this failed, they would use one or another of the medical contraceptives eleborately described by Soranos. If not-withstanding a woman became pregnant, she would try to abort. And if even this failed, there was always the Roman law that permitted infanticide."

[3] Noonan p. 438.

[4] From recent conversations with Msgr. William D. Smith, Professor of Moral Theology of St. Joseph Seminary, Yonkers, NY, who was privy to the twelve volumes of all the Acta (proceedings) of the Commission.

[5] John Kippley, Sex and the Marriage Covenant, (Cincinnati. OH, Couple to Couple League Publisher), p. 295. Also see "Humanae Vitae" (Boston, MA: NC News Service Translation, printed by The Daughters of St. Paul, 1968), Art. 6. (Emphasis added.)

[6] Vatican Council II, "Pastoral Constitution on the Church in the Modern World", #50, p. 255.

[7] Maclyn E. Wade, Phyllis McCarthy, et al., "A Randomized Prospective Study of the Use-Effectiveness of Two Methods of Natural Family Planning", American Journal of Obstetrics and Gynecology 141:4 (Oct. 15, 1981) pp.368-376, quoted in John Kippley, The Effectiveness of Natural Family Planning (Cincinnati, OH: The Couple to Couple League International, Inc.), p.3.

[8] Nora Aguilar, <u>No-Pill, No-Risk Birth Control</u>, A survey of 157 NFP couples showed a divorce rate of less than 1% (New York, Rawson Wade Publishers, Inc.) pp. 104-105. John Kippley, Director of the International Couple to Couple League, has found among 900 NFP teaching couples 1.3% of divorce. He estimates an overall divorce rate for NFP users between 2% and 5%.

[9] 48th edition (Montvale, NJ: Medical Economics Co., Inc., 1994), p. 1691. (Emphasis added.)

[10] Vatican Council II, "The Church Today," #51, p. 256.

[11] <u>Sexual Sterilization</u>, (Cincinnati, OH: Couple to Couple League International Inc., 1981).

[12] John Kippley, <u>Birth Control and Christian Discipleship</u> (Cincinnati, OH: Couple to Couple League International, Inc., 1985), pp. 2-6.

[13] Michael F. Valente, <u>Sex the Radical View of a Catholic Theologian</u> (New York: Bruce Publishing Company, 1970), p. 126, quoted by J. Kippley, <u>Birth Control and Christian Discipleship</u>, pp. 8-9 and footnote 30, p. 34.

[14] Deborah Franklin, "The Birth Control Bind", <u>Health Magazine</u>, Eric W. Schrier, ed., (San Francisco, CA: Hippocrates Partners Publishers, July/August, 1992), Vol.6, no. 4, p 52.

[15] John Kippley, <u>Sex and the Marriage Covenant</u>, in ch. 7 "Is the Teaching Infallible?" treats the question exhaustively; he concludes it is.

[16] John T. Noonan, Jr., <u>Contraception</u>, pp 430-432.

[17] Charles D. Provan, <u>The Bible and Birth Control</u>, (Monongahela, PA: Zimmer Printing, 1989), pp 61-92.

[18] Noonan, p. 76.

[19] George A. Kelly, ed., <u>Biblical Thoughts on Human Sexuality, Human Sexuality in Our Time</u>, (Boston: St. Paul Editions, 1979), pp 112-115, quoted by J. Kippley, <u>Sex and The Marriage Covenant, A Basis for Morality</u>, (Cincinnati, OH: Couple to Couple League International, Inc., 1991), pp. 310-314.

[20] Rev. B. Vawter, C.M., "Genesis" <u>A New Catholic Commentary on Holy Scripture</u>, (New York: Thomas Nelson, Inc. Publishers, 1975, Rev. Reginal Fuller, Gen. Ed.), p. 202. (Emphasis added.)

[21] Grand Rapids, MI: Zondervan Publishing House, 1961, p. 59. (Emphasis added.)

[22] Minneapolis, MN: Bethany House Publishers, 1977.

[23] <u>The Bible and Birth Control</u>, (Monongahela, PA: Zimmer Printing, 1989).

[24] Dear Pastor, leaflet, (Cincinnati, OH, The Couple to Couple League International, Inc.) (Emphasis added.)

Epilogue

[1] Fr. John Hardon, S.J., Address on The New Paganism, Human Life International Conference, Metairie, La., Nov. 20-22, 1992. Cassette available from HLI, 7845 E. Airpark Rd., Gaithersburg, MD, 20879.

[2] "The Unity of the Catholic Church", The Faith of the Early Fathers, p. 221 [6] #557.

[3] Eg. Jn 3:11 & Mt 25:40.

[4] Joachim Jeremias, New Testament Theology: The Proclamation of Jesus [Eng. translation] (New York, Charles Scribner's Sons 1971), p. 35-36. "A new use of the word 'amen' emerges in the sayings of Jesus in the four gospels, which is without any parallel in the whole of Jewish literature and the rest of the New Testament...'amen' is used, also without exception, to introduce and strengthen a person's own words; in this unprecedented usage it is strictly confined to the words of Jesus."

[5] Vatican Council II, pp 713-715. (Emphasis added.)

[6] Hardon, S.J., The New Paganism.

[7] Many of the thoughts in this paragraph were both corroborated and inspired by Fr. John Hardon's address The New Paganism.

Appendix

[1] Danforth's Obstetrics and Gynecology, 6th Edition, (Philadelphia PA: J.B. Lippincott Company, 1990), p. 713. (Emphasis added.)

[2] 48th Edition, (Montvale, NJ: Medical Economics Data, 1994), p. 1691. (Emphasis added.)

[3] Dr. and Mrs. J.C. Willke, Abortion, Questions and Answers (Cincinnati, OH: Hayes Publishing Company, 1991), p. 234. (Emphasis added.)

[4] Ibid., p. 235.

[5] U.S. Dept of HEW, Second Report on IUDs, Dec. 1978, Food and Drug Administration Document 017-012-00276-5.

[6] Rudolf Ehmann M.D., Dresden, Sept. 20 - 23, 1990, pp. 20-21. (Emphasis added.)

[7] "Norplant" is available from Pope Paul VI Institute, 6901 Mercy Rd., Omaha, NE 68106. (Emphasis added.)

[8] P. 2414. (Emphasis added.)

[9] Willke, M.D., p. 89. (Emphasis added.)

[10] Ehmann, M.D., p. 25.

[11] Willke, M.D., pp. 89-90.

[12] Maclyn E. Wade, Phyllis McCarthy, et al., "A Randomized Prospective Study of the Use Effectiveness of Two Methods of Natural Family Planning." <u>American Journal of Obstetrics and Gynecology</u> 141:4 (Oct. 15, 1981), pp. 368-376, quoted in John Kippley, <u>The Effectiveness of Natural Family Planning</u>, (Cincinnati, OH, Couple to Couple League International, Inc. 1986), p.3.

[13] Jacqueline Kasun, <u>War Against Population</u>, (San Francisco, CA: Ignatius Press, 1988) and <u>Population Control of The Family</u> (Gaithersburg, MD: Human Life International Booklet, 1988).

[14] Robert Sassone, <u>Handbook on Population</u>, (Santa Ana, CA: R.L. Sassone Publisher, 1978).

[15] Julian Simon, <u>Population Matters</u> (New Brunswick, NJ: Transaction Pub., 1990), <u>Ultimate Resource</u> (Princeton Univ. Press, 1981), <u>The Resourceful Earth: A Response to Global 2000</u> (with Herman Kahn) (Oxford, England: Basil Blackwell Inc., 1984).

[16] "The Unreported Revolution in Population Economics", (Washington, DC: The Public Interest, National Affairs, Inc., Fall 1990), p. 89. (Emphasis added.)

[17] <u>Project Population Myths</u>, (Gaithersburg, MD: HLI, June 1992).

[18] Kasun, <u>Population Control of The Family</u>, p. 5.

[19] <u>Project Population Myths</u>, p. 6.

[20] Ibid pp. 2-3.

[21] Kasun, <u>Population Control of the Family</u>, p. 6.

[22] <u>Population Research Institute Review</u> (Gaithersburg, MD: Human Life International, Sept.—Oct., 1991).

GIFT OF THE CHURCH

GIFT OF THE CHURCH

192